A STUDY OF FINANCIAL INCLUSION AND MANAGEMENT OF PERSONAL FINANCE

DR. SHAHINA QURESHI

To

My Father
Mr. Iftikhar Ahmed Qureshi

who always guided me with Love and Affection

Contents

Preface

As it is reported by Economists, Researchers and Scholars that Inclusive financial systems provide individuals and firms with greater access to resources to meet their financial needs, such as saving for retirement, investing in education, capitalizing on business opportunities, and confronting shocks. But in the Real-world, financial systems are far from inclusive. Indeed, half of the world's adult population lacks a bank account. Many of the world's poor would benefit from financial services but cannot access them due to market failures or inadequate public policies. This Study contributes new data and research that helps fill some of the gaps in knowledge about financial inclusion. It also draws on existing insights and experience to contribute to the policy discussion on this critical development issue. Financial inclusion has moved up the global reform agenda and become a topic of great interest for policy makers, regulators, researchers, market practitioners, and other stakeholders.

This Research Study throws light on the global financial development and growth. It deals with the present scenario of Financial Inclusion Worldwide. It discusses barriers to Financial Inclusion and provides fruitful insight to improve the financial position of the Countries. The present study also attempts to assess the financial inclusion in India and analyses the trends and patterns of economic inequality across Indian states. The basic objective here is to understand the dynamics of growth in the country which is resulting in regional imbalances and propose measures for alleviating the problem.

The present study is structured around ten chapters. A brief description of each chapter is as follows:

The first chapter highlights the nature and need of the financial inclusion in the process of inclusive growth and explains the importance of financial inclusion in India. This chapter also contains an exhaustive review of the existing literature pertaining to the area of research. The studies have been presented in chronological order so that the latest studies are presented first followed by the subsequent studies. Research gaps have been identified and a case for the present study has been built in the end. Research Methodology proposed to be adopted to fill the research gap has also been defined in this chapter. It defines the statement of problem and research objectives of the present study. It also provides insights into the framework to implement the research objectives of the present study. This chapter also outlines the research methodology employed, the way the data for the study has been collected and the statistical tools used for data analysis.

The Second Chapter is focused on the global reach of the financial sector—the extent of financial inclusion and the degree to which such groups as the poor, women, and youth are excluded from formal financial systems. The aim of this chapter is to throw light on the global financial development and growth. It deals with the present scenario of Financial Inclusion

Worldwide. It also discusses barriers to Financial Inclusion and provides fruitful insight to improve the financial position of the Countries.

The Third Chapter reviews the roles of technology, product design, financial capability, financial education programs, consumer protection and market conduct, and government policies in fostering financial inclusion.

The Fourth Chapter is focused on the status of financial inclusion in India. The purpose of this chapter is to present an outline of the concept of financial inclusion and its major milestones in India. It also deals with the present scenario of financial inclusion in India.

The Fifth Chapter discusses the relationship between financial inclusion and economic development of the country with the help of Index of Financial Inclusion and also explores the factors associated with financial inclusion with the help of Regression Analysis.

The Sixth Chapter analyses the trends and patterns of economic inequality across the Indian states. The basic objective here is to understand the dynamics of growth in the country which is resulting in regional imbalances and proposes measures for alleviating the problem. The inter-state inequality in bank branches, credit accounts, saving accounts and credit deposit ratio show a clear picture of regional inequality in India.

The Seventh Chapter critically evaluates the initiatives taken by the Reserve Bank of India for attaining of financial inclusion. The Eighth Chapter discusses the issues and challenges being faced by banks for achieving a better level

of Financial Inclusion in India. The conclusion and suggestions emerging from present research are explained in the Chapter Nine. Limitations of the study and further scope of research area is explained in this chapter.
-Shahina Qureshi

Acknowledgements

In the Name of Allah, the Most Beneficent, the Most Merciful

First of all, I would like to express my special thanks to Allah Subhana Wa Tallah for helping me at every stage of research development. He is the creator who created me for the betterment of society and supported me like a partner and a good friend, whenever I needed Allah He supported me in a very miraculous way and made all things possible, and my Heavenly Father Late Mr. Iftikhar Ahmed Qureshi for giving me the strength, bestowing upon me the courage to face the complexities of life and complete this project successfully.

I have to acknowledge that the pursuit of my Ph.D. is not a solo journey. During the three years of my study as a doctoral student, I had the opportunity to gain knowledge and share experiences with different stakeholders who contributed a lot to enrich my thoughts as a researcher. I am grateful to all of them and it is now a pleasure for me to acknowledge their contributions.

I would like to express my profound gratitude and moral indebtedness to my Co-supervisor Prof. Dr. P. N. Mishra, Director & Professor, Institute of Management Studies (IMS), Indore for his dedicated and aspiring mentorship, intellectual guidance, and wise counseling right from conceptualizing the research proposal till the preparation of this thesis. Enduring this long journey would not have been possible without his encouragement and guidance.

Undoubtedly, this research could not have been conceived and realized without the support of my Supervisor Dr. Vinay Goyal, Professor, Indian Institute of Management (IIM), Raipur who provide me with valuable guidance and motivation and principally helped me in the completion of my dissertation. I owe my special thanks to him for his guidance in the research design and statistical analysis of the study.

A person can peacefully progress only when there is support from his family. I am lucky to have such a family which supported and facilitated my pursuit of academic activities overlooking other responsibilities. Many thanks to all of them- My Babuji, Ammi, My Brothers-Shoaib Bhai, Waqar, & Rameez, My Sisters-

Shabina & Shimail, without their support this research would not have been in its present structure and style. They were always present for valuable feedback and criticism to develop good research. Finally, I wish to thank a very special person Mohammed Misbah who had been critical and constructive on the first cut of the research document. I acknowledge his valuable contribution to the final form of a research thesis. His motivation and inspiration helped me to accomplish my objectives. One of the greatest pieces of advice given by the Prophet Muhammad (Peace Be Upon Him) was: "The most beloved actions to Allah are those performed consistently, even if they are few". This statement kept ringing in my mind and reminded me all the time that as a Researcher I need to do my best for society.

-Shahina Qureshi

CHAPTER ONE

Introduction to Financial Inclusion

Ever since the first Financial Development Report was printed, global leaders have mounted an extraordinary response to a financial crisis, the effects of which have wrinkled across all regions and levels of society. The exigency of the threat to the global economy and our collective prosperity has required pragmatic and at times inventive responses that transcended the conventions of recent history. As with past crises and episodes of dramatic change, decisions made now have the potential to impact generations to come. New models for global governance and cooperation are needed that are commensurate with the realities of increasing financial integration and economic interdependence. As dialogue and consensus develop on new models for global financial governance, it is vital to bring a balanced and rich perspective to bear on these decisions. It is not only the more visible decisions at the global level that matter but also those taken at the regional and local levels, which have the potential to build stronger financial systems that help extend prosperity to all. The Financial Development Report, in providing a depth of information across a number of economies, serves to highlight some of the variation across individual financial systems that must be considered in building on existing strengths and looking for workable solutions to problems. Once the priorities of stabilization have been achieved, reform and development must be undertaken with sensitivity to the requirements, levels of development, and specific circumstances of individual countries. The stability of financial systems must certainly be a central factor, but effective corporate governance, robust legal regimes promoting contract enforcement, availability of human capital, and other factors are also critical to nurturing competitive and resilient financial systems. For policymakers charged with the overall economic welfare of the broader population, how do they ensure that the financial system serves all constituencies, including those that are less privileged? The measures of financial access capture in the index of financial development illustrate that even while large corporations may have relatively easy availability of capital in particular markets; small enterprises and individuals in the same countries may not. Governments need to be quite nuanced in their approaches to ensure that financial markets can support innovation and growth at all levels of society. It is crucial that development areas within these financial systems be addressed to ensure that future economic growth is not undermined: new sources of long-term capital must be tapped to fund much-needed infrastructure; local capital markets must be developed to meet the expanding credit needs of all economic sectors; and access to retail financial services must be extended to help stimulate consumer demand in these markets, which in turn can offset global imbalances.

A specific challenge will be to instill financial stability without having the negative side-effect of inhibiting economic growth. Improvement efforts need to be driven by local level reforms to ensure that the appropriate financial systems are in place, thereby helping extend prosperity to all. Thus, the countries have to identify and develop workable solutions for building on existing strengths and addressing potential problematic areas.

The Financial Development Report 2011 and the Financial Development Index ("the Index") on which it is based provide a score and rank for 60 of the world's leading financial systems and capital markets. The Index analyzes drivers of financial system development that support economic growth. Ultimately, it aims to serve as a tool for both advanced and emerging economies to benchmark themselves and thereby to identify and prioritize areas for reform.

The Report defines *financial development as the factors, policies, and institutions that lead to effective financial intermediation and markets, as well as deep and broad access to capital and financial services.* In accordance with this definition, measures of financial development are captured across the seven pillars of the Index:

1. **Institutional environment:** encompasses financial sector liberalization, corporate governance, legal and regulatory issues, and contract enforcement.
2. **Business environment:** considers human capital, taxes, infrastructure, and costs of doing business.
3. **Financial stability:** captures the risk of currency crises, systemic banking crises, and sovereign debt crises.
4. **Banking financial services:** measures size, efficiency, and financial disclosure.
5. **Non-banking financial services:** includes IPO and M&A activity, insurance, and securitization.
6. **Financial markets:** contains foreign exchange and derivative markets, and equity and bond market development.
7. **Financial access:** evaluates commercial and retail access.

The Index takes a holistic view in assessing the factors that contribute to the long-term development of financial systems. Such an approach will allow decision makers to develop a balanced perspective when determining which aspects of their country's financial system are most important, and to calibrate this view empirically relative to other countries. As the global financial system moves from crisis to crisis, it is tempting for international leaders to focus all reform efforts on restoring stability to the system.

Financial systems play a vital role in economic development and, to be successful in the longer term, countries must take a holistic view by identifying and improving long-term factors that are crucial to their development. Such a process would allow countries to encourage economic prosperity for all participants in the global economy. This approach is supported by empirical studies that have generally found that cross-country differences in levels of financial development explain a considerable portion of the cross-country differences in growth rates of economies. A large body of economic literature supports the premise that, in addition to many other important factors, the performance and long-run economic growth and welfare of a country are related to its degree of financial development. Financial development is measured by factors such as size, depth, access, and the efficiency and stability of a financial system, which includes its markets, intermediaries, range of assets, institutions, and regulations. The higher the degree of financial development, the wider the availability of financial services that allows the diversification of risks. This increases the long-run growth trajectory of a country and ultimately improves the welfare and prosperity of producers and consumers with access to financial services. The link between financial development and economic growth can be traced back to the work of Joseph Schumpeter in the early 20th century.

With the winds of economic liberalization and globalization, the banking sector all over the world is re-adjusting its procedures, practices, services, and functioning for meeting the new challenges. They are making conscious choices from the alternatives for achieving high growth and socioeconomic objectives. Even otherwise, in today's hi-fi and speedy innovative world, no bank can continue to do what it has been doing for very long. Every bank has either to do new things or do the same things differently by evolving and adopting a strategy of innovating creativity to balance their socio-economic and commercial interests.

In this regard, it has come up exclusively on financial inclusion. As a concept, financial inclusion may be new for many readers, but its practice has a long history in economic development. It has been a major implied fact of the theories and strategies of balanced growth. Across the globe, the planners and politicians have been advocating directly or indirectly the concept of financial inclusion. In India, too, it has a long history. But its application as an economic development strategy remained quite narrow, slow and sectoral. The major impetus to financial inclusion was given in 1969 when 14 banks were nationalized. Since then, its coverage has been expanding continuously. But still, the target of inclusion is far away from the ideal position.

Financial inclusion has moved up the global reform agenda and become a topic of great interest for policy makers, regulators, researchers, market practitioners, and other stakeholders. For the World Bank Group, financial inclusion represents a core topic, given its implications for reducing poverty and boosting shared prosperity. The increased emphasis on financial inclusion reflects a growing realization of its potentially transformative power to accelerate development gains. Inclusive financial systems provide individuals and firms with greater access to resources to meet their financial needs, such as saving for retirement, investing in education, capitalizing on business opportunities, and confronting shocks. Real-world financial systems are far from inclusive. Indeed, half of the world's adult population lacks a bank account. Many of the world's poor would benefit from financial services but cannot access them due to market failures or inadequate public policies.

Financial inclusion-typically defined as the proportion of individuals and firms that use financial services has become a subject of considerable interest among policy makers, researchers, and other stakeholders. In international forums, such as the Group of Twenty (G-20), financial inclusion has moved up the reform agenda. At the country level, about two-thirds of regulatory and supervisory agencies are now charged with enhancing financial inclusion. In recent years, some 50 countries have set formal targets and goals for financial inclusion.

The heightened interest reflects a better understanding of the importance of financial inclusion for economic and social development. It indicates a growing recognition that access to financial services has a critical role in reducing extreme poverty, boosting shared prosperity, and supporting inclusive and sustainable development. The interest also derives from a growing recognition of the large gaps in financial inclusion. For example, half of the world's adult population-more than 2.5 billion people—do not have an account at a formal financial institution. Some of this nonuse demonstrates lack of demand, but barriers such as cost, travel distance, and amount of paperwork play a key part. It is encouraging that most of these barriers can be reduced by better policies.

Indeed, some progress has been achieved. For example, in South Africa, 6 million basic bank accounts were opened in four years, significantly increasing the share of adults with a bank account. Worldwide, hundreds of millions have gained access to electronic payments through services using mobile phone platforms. In the World Bank's Global Financial Barometer (ˇCihák 2012; World Bank 2012a), 78 percent of the financial sector practitioners surveyed indicated that, in their assessment, access to finance in their countries had improved substantially in the last five years.

But boosting financial inclusion is not trivial. Creating new bank accounts does not always translate into regular use. For example, of the above-mentioned 6 million new accounts in South Africa, only 3.5 million became active, while the rest lie dormant. Moreover, things can go—and do go—badly, especially if credit starts growing rapidly. The promotion of credit without sufficient regard for financial stability is likely to result in a crisis. A spectacular recent example is the subprime mortgage crisis in the United States in the 2000s: the key contributing factors included the overextension of credit to non-creditworthy borrowers and relaxation in mortgage-underwriting standards. Another example of overextension of credit in the name of access was the crisis in India's microfinance sector in 2010. Because of a rapid growth in loans, India's microfinance institutions were able to report high profitability for years, but this resided on large indebtedness among clients. While these two examples are more complex, they illustrate the broader point that deep social issues cannot be resolved purely with an infusion of credit. If not implemented properly, efforts to promote financial inclusion can lead to defaults and other negative effects.

Lack of accessible, affordable and appropriate financial services has always been a global problem. It is estimated that about 2.9 billion people around the world do not have access to formal sources of banking and financial services. India is said to live in its villages, a convincing statement, considering that nearly 72% of our population lives there. However, a significant proportion of our 6, 50,000 odd villages do not have a single bank branch to boast of, leaving swathes of the rural population in financial exclusion. RBI has reported that the financial exclusion in India leads to the loss of GDP to the extent of one per cent (RBI, Working Paper Series (DEPR): 8/2011). Financially excluded people, consistently, depend on money lenders even for their day to day needs, borrowing at excessive rates to finally get caught in a debt trap. In addition, people in far-off villages are completely unaware of financial products like insurance, which could protect them in adverse situation. Therefore, financial inclusion is a big necessity for our country as a large chunk of the world's poor resides here. Access to finance by the poor and vulnerable groups is a prerequisite for poverty reduction and social cohesion.

Even after 60 years of independence, a large section of Indian population still remains unbanked. This malaise has led generation of financial instability among the lower income group who do not have access to financial products and services. However, in the recent years the government and Reserve Bank of India have been pushing the concept and idea of financial inclusion.

The Government of India and the Reserve Bank of India have been making concerted efforts to promote financial inclusion as one of the important national objectives of the country. Some of the major efforts made in the last five decades including - nationalization of banks, building up of robust branch network of scheduled commercial banks, co-operatives and regional rural banks, introduction of mandated priority sector lending targets, lead bank scheme, formation of self-help groups, permitting BCs/BFs to be appointed by banks to provide door step delivery of banking services, zero balance BSBD accounts, etc. The fundamental objective of all these initiatives is to provide the financial services to the large section of the hitherto financially excluded Indian population.

Government of India and RBI have taken various steps to include vast segment of unbanked people in to mainstream banking such as Micro Finance- Self Help Group Model (1992), Kisan Credit Card (1998), No Frill Accounts (2004), Business Correspondents and Business Facilitators (2006, 2009) Swabhimaan (2011) financial inclusion model but the path of financial inclusion is continuous to be challenging. The United Nations (UN) had raised the basic question, "Why so many bankable people in rural and urban areas are unbanked?" NSSO data revealed that 45.9 million farmer households in the country (51.4 per cent), out of a total of 89.3 million households do not access credit, either from institutional or non institutional sources. Various financial experts argue that bank account is the most basic step of bringing such people under financial mainstream. So the primary objective of financial inclusion should be to open bank accounts of unbanked people. These people have remained aloof from financial and banking mainstream and they don‘t possess bank account, don‘t have knowledge about financial and saving instruments and are unable to reap benefits on whatever large or small amount of money they have at their disposal. In simple language financial inclusion stands for including the people lying on the lowest strata of our social pyramid into the financial mainstream.

But financial inclusion also implies a very important point. It is felt that a majority of the unbanked people are not used to frills, now normally associated with modern banking. These people require the most basic banking facilities which are free of frills. That means financial inclusion is no-frill banking. The policy makers have already initiated some positive measures aimed at expanding financial inclusion. However, the efforts are opined by many as not commensurate with the magnitude of the issue. There is also a need on the part of the academicians and researchers to study the issue of financial inclusion with a comprehensive approach in order to highlight its need and importance.

By financial inclusion, we mean delivery of financial services, including banking services and credit at an affordable cost to the vast sections of disadvantaged and low income groups. The concept of financial inclusion is not new in India. The concept has been prevailing in India from past 44 years. Beginning with the nationalization of commercial banks in 1969 and 1980, another major step taken was the establishment of Regional Rural Banks in 1975 and banking sector reforms after 1991. As a result of these three major policy changes, the numbers of branches of commercial bank have increased from 8262 in June 1969 to 102343 in 2013 (Economic survey 2012-2013) and population per branches decline rapidly from 65000 to 13756 (RBI 2008).

Financial inclusion is a very useful tool for financial growth of India. When compared to the developed world, the coverage of our financial services is quite low. Then the Reserve Bank of India has set up a commission (Khan Commission) in 2004 to look into financial inclusion and the recommendations of the commission were incorporated into the mid-term review of the policy (2005–06). In the report RBI exhorted the banks with a view of achieving greater financial inclusion to make available a basic "no-frills" banking account. In India, Financial Inclusion first featured in 2005, when it was introduced, that, too, from a pilot project in UT of Pondicherry, by K C Chakrabarty, the Chairman of Indian Bank. Mangalam Village became the first village in India where all households were provided banking facilities. In addition to this KYC (Know Your Customer) norms were relaxed for people intending to open accounts with annual deposits of less than 50,000 rupees. General Credit Cards (GCC) were issued to the poor and the disadvantaged with a view to help them access easy credit.

Financial inclusion is the process of ensuring access to appropriate financial products and services needed by vulnerable groups such as weaker sections and low income groups at an affordable cost. Reserve Bank of India in collaboration with the Government of India had formulated a policy namely Financial Inclusion Policy (2005) for financially including of the excluded. The policy was framed with the objective of employment generation, asset creation and income increase which would help in the upliftment of the weaker or poor people. Formal financial institutions, NGOs and SHGs help in the inclusive growth through financially including the low income and weaker section of the population.

Financial inclusion is the delivery of financial services at affordable costs to sections of disadvantaged and low income segments of society. It is argued that as banking services are in the nature of public good, it is essential that availability of banking and payment services to the entire population without discrimination is the prime objective of public policy. The objective of financial inclusion is to deliver banking services at an affordable cost to vast sections of the low-income groups. Indian Finance Minister has set the ball rolling by articulating the Government's decision to provide essential financial services like savings, credit, micro insurance and remittance, for all villages with population over 2,000 by March 2012.

Financial Inclusion is a process or concept formulated with an objective of providing financial products and services to every constituent of our society, especially economically backward people. This concept has been developed and implemented keeping in mind the mainstream banking service providers. This is because it was felt that burden of financial services to downtrodden and poor people has been made a prerogative of rural banks and cooperative banks, who are not the mainstream players. And if mainstream players are not involved in this initiative it would be the traditional quasi banking establishments, who would again take undue benefit of this situation.

Financial inclusion also includes the objective of providing cheap loans to the most downtrodden people because their essential requirement from banking system is get access to funds to sustain their livelihood.

Financial inclusion has indeed far reaching positive consequences, which can facilitate many people to come out of the abject poverty conditions. It is widely believed that financial inclusion provides formal identity, access to payments system and deposit insurance, and many other financial services. Universally, it is accepted that the objective of financial inclusion is to extend the scope of activities of the organized financial system to include within its ambit the people with low incomes. In India, there is a need for coordinated action amongst the banks, the government and related agencies to facilitate access to bank accounts to the financially excluded. In view of the need for further financial deepening in the country in order to boost economic development, there is a dire need for expanding financial inclusion. By expanding financial inclusion, inclusive growth can be attained by achieving equity.

Financial inclusion may be defined as the process of ensuring access to financial services and timely and adequate credit where needed by vulnerable groups such as weaker sections and low income groups at an affordable cost (The Committee on Financial Inclusion, Chairman: Dr. C. Rangarajan). Financial Inclusion, broadly defined, refers to universal access to a wide range of financial services at a reasonable cost. These include not only banking products but also other financial services such as insurance and equity products (The Committee on Financial Sector Reforms, Chairman: Dr. Raghuram G. Rajan).

Financial inclusion means and includes delivery of financial services at an affordable cost to the vast sections of the disadvantaged and low-income groups in a given society. Access to finance by the poor and vulnerable groups is a prerequisite for achieving inclusive growth in any given economic system. The entire world economies try varied methods and mechanism to achieve this. Their experiences are so different from each other that they provide valuable reference points and help as practical examples. However, they point out the need for country specific studies, as Financial Inclusion depends on the social and economic conditions which vary from country to country. The need for working towards complete financial inclusion is more pronounced that it has become rather a compulsion than a choice in emerging economies like India. Financial Inclusion basically measures the efficacy in which financial resources are pooled and bartered. Simply stated that it covers the financial literacy level of the population, their banking habits, and the coverage of the entire financial system.

The United Nations Secretary-General's Special Advocate for Inclusive Finance for Development (UNSGSA) defines financial inclusion as universal access to, and use of, to a wide range of reasonably priced financial services, provided by a variety of sound and sustainable institutions. Financial inclusion is an enabler and accelerator of economic growth, job creation and development. Affordable access to, and use of, financial services helps families and small enterprise owners generate income, manage irregular cash flow, invest in opportunities, strengthen resilience to shocks, and work their way out of poverty.

Various financial services would include access to savings, loans, insurance, payments and remittance facilities by the formal financial system to those who tend to be excluded. Savings and investments help in poverty alleviation and also add to GDP growth in any economy. But accessing of formal financial system is still a distant dream to a vast section all over the world, and India is not an exception to it. One of the key financial services that is of great relevance here is that of risk management or risk mitigation services visa-a vise economic shocks which may be an income shock via loss of income due to adverse weather conditions or natural disasters or an expenditure shock due to health emergencies or accidents leading to a high level of unexpected expenditure.

This aspect of financial inclusion is of vital importance in providing economic security to individuals and families. Financial inclusion is important simply because it is a necessary condition for sustaining equitable growth. There are few, if any, instances of an economy transiting from an agrarian system to post-industrial modern society without broad-based financial inclusion. As people having comfortable access to financial services, economic opportunity is strongly intertwined with financial access. Such access is especially powerful for the poor as it provides them the opportunity to build savings, make investments and avail credit. Importantly, access to financial services also helps the poor insure themselves against income shocks and equips them to meet emergencies such as illness, death in the family or loss of employment. Needless to add, financial inclusion protects the poor from the clutches of the usurious money-lenders. Financial inclusion will make it possible for governments to make payments such as social security transfers, National Rural Employment Guarantee Programme (NREGA) wages in the bank accounts of beneficiaries through the Electric Benefit Transfers (EBT) method. This will minimize transaction costs including leakages. In parts of the country where such EBT has already taken off, the results are impressive and the experience of both payers and recipients is extremely satisfying. There are enormous benefits at the aggregate level too. The first and more obvious benefit is that financial inclusion provides an avenue for bringing the savings of the poor in to the formal financial intermediation system and channelizes them into investments. Second, the large number of low cost deposits will offer banks and opportunity to reduce their dependencies on bulk deposits and help them to better manage both liquidity risk and asset-liability mismatches.

Financial Exclusion

The term financial exclusion was first coined in 1993 by geographers who were concerned about limited physical access to banking services as a result of bank branch closures (Leyshon and Thrift, 1993). Throughout the 1990s there was also a growing body of research relating to difficulties faced by some sections of societies in gaining access to modern payment instruments and other banking services, to consumer credit and to insurance. There was also concern about some people lacking savings of any kind. It was in 1999, that the term financial exclusion seems first to have been used in a broader sense to refer to people who have constrained access to mainstream financial services (Kempson and Whyley, 1999). Since then, a number of commentators have added their views of how financial exclusion should be defined. These include both academics (for example, Anderloni, 2003; Anderloni and Carluccio, 2006; Carbo et al, 2004; Devlin, 2005; Gloukoviezoff, 2004; Kempson et al, 2000; Sinclair, 2001); and policy makers (Treasury Committee, 2006a, 2006b; HM Treasury, 2004).

The general consensus is that it refers to people who have difficulty accessing appropriate financial services and products in the mainstream financial services market. Two aspects of this definition are important: First the reference to appropriate products and secondly to the mainstream financial services market – as much of the exclusion appears to arise from a failure of the mainstream commercial providers to supply a range of products and services that are appropriate to the needs of all sections of society.

Financial exclusion leads to social exclusion. The excluded section comprise of the marginal farmers, landless laborers, self employed, and unorganized sector, enterprises, urban slum dwellers, migrants, ethnic minorities and socially excluded group, senior citizens and women (Rangarajan Committee Report).

There is also a widespread recognition that financial exclusion forms part of a much wider social exclusion, faced by some groups who lack access to quality essential services such as jobs, housing, education or health care. The policies for tackling financial exclusion offers integrated solutions for social exclusion also (Marshal 2004).

Financial exclusion is, however, a complex concept and the following key issues need to be considered:

- Exclusion from which financial services and institutions?
- Do we need to draw a distinction between access to financial services and usage of them?
- Are there degrees of financial exclusion and, if so, how to express these?

- For whom do we measure access: the individual, the family or the household?

Today, 2.5 billion adults—more than a third of the world's population—are excluded from the formal financial system. Financial exclusion is greatest among poor people and in emerging and developing countries, including the rural households that account for more than 70% of global poverty. This hampers people's ability to earn, protect themselves in times of crisis, and to build for the future. In addition, more than 200 million formal SMEs in emerging markets alone lack access to finance, limiting their ability to grow and thrive.

Are there degrees of financial exclusion?

There are two aspects to be considered in this regard. First, as we discussed earlier, people may have varying levels of engagement with banking services. So they may have a deposit account but not a transaction one. They may have access to some, but not all the transaction banking facilities that would be appropriate to their circumstances. It is for this reason, that the terms unbanked, marginally (or under-) banked and fully banked have been coined (Anderloni and Carluccio, 2006; BMRB, 2006; Barr, 2004; Corr, 2006; Kempson, 2006).

There is, however, another important dimension to this debate which is the extent to which people has access to transaction banking services but not through mainstream providers – in this case the banks and other similar organizations. In some countries there are a range of alternative providers or fringe banks that cater to the needs of people without a transaction bank account. These include organizations specializing in offering cheque cashing, bill-payment or remittance services. Generally, people who use these are considered unbanked if they lack a transaction bank account or marginally banked if they have one but do not use it (Barr, 2004; Caskey, 1994; Kempson and Whyley, 1999).

Likewise some people may be able to get a cash loan from a high cost sub-prime lender but not an overdraft or a credit card in the prime credit market, while others might be denied all forms of credit, even in the sub-prime market. Both are usually considered credit excluded but the term 'completely credit excluded' has only been used to describe the second of these two groups (Kempson and Collard, 2005).

Financial Inclusion-Inclusive Growth Model

The concept of inclusive growth has gained wide importance in several countries including India (Bolt, 2004). Inclusive growth implies participation in the process of growth and also sharing of benefit from growth. Growth is considered to be pro-poor as long as poor benefit in absolute terms, as reflected in some agreed measure of poverty (Ravallion and Chen, 2003). Growth with equity is the only road to success. It has been globally recognized that high national income growth alone does not address the challenge of employment promotion, poverty reduction and balanced regional development. Nor does growth in itself improve human development. Consequently, all the efforts of government – in agricultural and rural development, in industry and urban development, in infrastructure and services, in education and health care – sought to promote inclusive growth.

Financial inclusion is an important step towards inclusive growth. It helps in the overall economic development of the disadvantaged population. Financial inclusion is also considered to be a business opportunity for the formal financial institutions. It would help them in penetrating into unbanked areas and thereby attaining profit. Besides the bankers, the developmental authorities also have a major role in developing the supportive infrastructure, both physical and social. Literacy, health and communication are some of the essential ingredients needed for inclusive growth. To conclude, the four pillars of inclusive growth are productivity, employment, financial inclusion and infrastructure development.

A rapidly modernizing economy needs effective social, economical and financial policies for those who had left behind. From 2006-2010, the growth rate was arranged at 8.6 per cent making India as one of fastest growing economies in the world, but the growth is not equitable. The Eleventh Five Year (2007-2011) Plan provides "an opportunity to restructure policies to achieve a new vision based on faster, more broad based and inclusive growth. It is designed to reduce poverty and focus on bringing the various divides that continue to fragment our society" (GOI, 2006: 1). The policies aim at increasing the income and employment opportunities on the one hand and on the other hand it tries to finance programmes which are capable of making the growth more inclusive.

Rural areas, where 70 per cent of Asia's poor live, continue to lag behind and the reasons identified were (1) limited access to financial services; (2) poor infrastructure, notably power, transport, and communications; (3) limited information about market opportunities; (4) a lack of education and training; and (5) limited access to new technologies, including information and communication technology. Hence greater efforts are required for them to participate in inclusive growth. Inclusive growth as the literal meaning of the two words refers to both the pace and the pattern of the economic growth. The inclusive growth approach is long term in nature which focuses on the productive employment which increases the means of incomes of the excluded section. Inclusive growth allows people to contribute and to get benefit from economic growth. The eleventh five year plan (2007-2012) envisions inclusive growth as the key objective.

Financial inclusion helps in striking a balance by channelizing the surplus to deficit units and brings the poor and disadvantaged one under the growth allegory. The concept —Inclusion‖ should be seen as a process of including the excluded as agents whose participation is essential in the very design of the development process, and not simply as welfare targets of development programme (Planning Commission, 2007).

The focus of economic policy in India has shifted to issues of equitable growth. This implies that the economy should not only maintain the tempo of growth but also spread the benefits of growth to all sections of the population of the country. In India, where rapid economic growth has become a national goal, analysis of the sources of growth assumes special importance to formulation of the macroeconomic strategy and policies that affect the future growth rate. This change in approach is significant for the hilly regions of the country, as they constantly struggle with underdevelopment, even when the rest of the economy is doing well. There has been a significant shift in the focus of economic policy in India in the last few years, with issues of equitable growth getting more importance. This is clearly revealed in the change in the Planning Commission's perspective – from high growth during the Tenth Five Year Plan to inclusive growth in its Approach Paper to the Eleventh Five-Year Plan. With sustained fertility decline and growing survival chances, India is likely to face many new challenges in the realm of its population management strategies especially those relating to life situations or the quality of human life and their key socio-economic determinants. Some of the economic literature clearly indicates a growing strain on many of these factors affecting the quality of human life and its determinants. Such literature and data sources also highlight the disparities and emerging mismatch between the post liberalization high GDP growth in the country and the quality of life experienced by a large segment of population in India (Dev and Ravi, 2007; UNICEF, 2005; NSS 61st round).

Financial Inclusion is the process of ensuring access to appropriate financial products and services needed by all sections of the society in general and vulnerable groups such as weaker sections and low income groups in particular at an affordable cost in a fair and transparent manner by mainstream institutional players. The States like Bihar, Orissa, Rajasthan Uttar Pradesh, Chhattisgarh, Jharkhand, West Bengal and North-Eastern States are under-banked.

According to the UK Financial Inclusion Taskforce, there are three main concerns in financial inclusion; access to banking, access to affordable credit and access to free face-to-face financial advice.

Access to safe, easy and affordable credit and other financial services by the poor and vulnerable groups, disadvantaged areas and lagging sectors is recognized as a precondition for accelerating growth and reducing income disparities and poverty. Access to a well-functioning financial system, by creating equal opportunities, enables economically and socially excluded people to integrate better into the economy and actively contribute to development and protects themselves against economic shocks. Despite the broad international consensus regarding the importance of access to finance as a crucial poverty alleviation tool, it is estimated that globally over two billion people are currently excluded from access to financial services (United Nations, 2006a). In most developing countries, a large segment of society, particularly low-income people, has very little access to financial services, both formal and semi-formal. As a consequence, many of them have to necessarily depend either on their own or informal sources of finance and generally at an unreasonably high cost. The situation is worse in most least developed countries (LDCs), where more than 90 per cent of the population is excluded from access to the formal financial system (United Nations, 2006a).

Important features of Financial Inclusion

a. Financial inclusion means the process of availing a minimum set of financial and banking services to the people residing in the lowest ladder of social paradigm
b. Financial inclusion presses upon including the mainstream banking and financial initiatives in this initiative
c. Opening a bank account is the most popular and simple tool of attaining objectives of financial inclusion
d. Financial inclusion is being promoted as an important tool to achieve the target of "sustainable growth"
e. Mangalam village of Puducherry became the first village to achieve 100 per cent financial inclusion

Factors Affecting Access to Financial Services

Financial Inclusion, on the one hand, is a process aiming at providing banking services like saving account, credit facility, and insurance product to weaker sections of the society. While on the other hand, it refers to the objective of ensuring financial services (banking, insurance, and capital market services) and timely and adequate credit to every section of the society as well as of the economy. Access to financial services has been recognized as an important aspect of development and more emphasis is given to extending financial services to low-income households as the poor lack the education and knowledge needed to understand financial services that are available to them. The lack of financial access limits the range of services and credits for household and enterprises. Although there is some evidence that access is improving but still there are multiple factors which have affected the access to financial services.

-Gender Issues

Access to credit is often limited for women who do not have, or cannot hold title to assets such as land and property or must seek male guarantees to borrow.

-Age Factor

Financial service providers usually target the middle of the economically active population, often overlooking the design of appropriate products for older or younger potential customers.

-Legal Identity

Lack of legal identities like identity cards, birth certificates or written records often exclude women, ethnic minorities, economic and political refugees and migrant workers from accessing financial services.

-Limited literacy

Limited literacy, particularly financial literacy, i.e., basic mathematics, business finance skills as well as lack of understanding, often constraints demand for financial services.

-Place of living

Although effective distance is as much about transportation infrastructure as physical distance, factors like density of population, rural and remote areas, mobility of the population (i.e., highly mobile people with no fixed or formal address), insurgency in a location, etc., also affect access to financial services.

-Psychological and cultural barriers

The feeling that banks are not interested to look into their cause has led to self exclusion for many of the low income groups. However, cultural and religious barriers to banking have also been observed in some of the country's Social security payments.

-Bank charges

In most of the countries, transaction is free as long as the account has sufficient funds to cover the cost of transactions made. However, there is a range of other hidden charges that have a disproportionate effect on people with low income.

-Terms and Conditions

Terms and conditions attached to products such as minimum balance requirements and conditions relating to the use of accounts often dissuade people from using such products/services.

-Level of Income

Financial status of people is always important in gaining access to financial services. Extremely poor people find it impossible to access financial services even when the services are made for them. Perception barriers and income discrimination among potential members in group-lending programmes may exclude the poorer members of the community.

-Type of occupation

Many banks have not developed the capacity to evaluate loan applications of small borrowers and unorganized enterprises and hence tend to deny such loan requests.

-Attractiveness of the Product

Both the financial services/products (savings accounts, credit products, payment services and insurance) and how their availability is marketed are crucial in financial inclusion.

According to Report on Currency and Finance 2006-08 the critical dimensions of Financial exclusion include access exclusion, condition exclusion (conditions attached to financial products), price exclusion and self exclusion because of the fear of refusal to access by the service providers. The financial exclusion process becomes self reinforcing and can often be an important factor in social exclusion, especially for communities with limited access to financial products, particularly in rural areas.

One of the successes in the last few years is supposed to have been the Mahatma Gandhi National Rural employment Guarantee Scheme. It has increased financial inclusion because it is mandated into the scheme that payments are made through the job cards, through bank accounts. Prior to this scheme of 'No frills accounts', as directed by the RBI, paved the way for Financial Inclusion. It is mandatory for state agencies to make the payments under various social security schemes through bank account.

Committees on Financial Inclusion (CFI)

Financial inclusion, of late, has become the business world in academic research, public policy meetings and seminars drawing wider attention in view of its important role in aiding economic development of the resource poor developing economies. In the Indian scenario, the term "financial inclusion" is popular in financial circles, especially after the Reserve Bank of India (RBI) announced a series of measures in its credit policy for 2006-07 to include many of the hitherto excluded groups in the banking net.

Government of India constituted a Committee to enhance financial inclusion in India on 22 June 2006. The Committee presented its report in January 2008. The report has analyzed financial inclusion in detail. CFI has initiated a mission called National Rural Financial Inclusion plan. It has set targets to increase FI in the country across regions and across institutions (banks, rural regional banks etc). It has suggested measures to address both, supply and demand constraints in increasing financial inclusion. The report suggested measures to address demand constraints in all the other forms of capital as well. To address human capital it stressed on health and education; for natural capital - enhance access to land which could provide collateral; for physical capital- improve infrastructure; social capital- develop institutions like gram panchayats etc.

The interim report was presented before the Budget (2007-08). The Finance Minister in the Budget decided to implement, immediately, two recommendations. The first was to establish a Financial Inclusion Fund with NABARD for meeting the cost of developmental and promotional interventions. The second was to establish a Financial Inclusion Technology Fund to meet the costs of technology adoption. The overall corpus for each fund was Rs.500 crore, with initial funding to be contributed by the Central Government, RBI and NABARD. In the 2008-09-budget statement, the Finance Minister proposed two more measures: one to add at least 250 rural household accounts every year at each of their rural and semi-urban branches of commercial banks (including regional rural banks) and two, to allow individuals such as retired bank officers, ex-servicemen etc to be appointed as business facilitator or business correspondent or credit counselor. The Finance Minister also proposed to expand the reach of NABARD, SIDBI and NHB. According to Indian institute of banking and finance, "financial inclusion is delivery of banking services at an affordable cost ('no frills' accounts,) to the vast sections of disadvantaged and low income group. Unrestrained access to public goods and services is the sine qua non of an open and efficient society. As banking services are in the nature of public good, it is essential that availability of banking and payment services to the entire population without discrimination is the prime objective of the public policy."

According to Dr. K.C. Chakrabarty, Deputy Governor, Reserve Bank of India, financial Inclusion is the process of ensuring access to appropriate financial products and services needed by all sections of the society in general and vulnerable groups such as weaker sections and low income groups in particular at an affordable cost in a fair and transparent manner by mainstream institutional players.

The Reserve Bank of India (RBI) constituted a committee under SH Khan to give recommendations on Financial Inclusion. On recommendations of this committee, RBI appealed to all commercial banks to come out with a no-frill bank account that would attract the downtrodden unbanked masses of the country for its simplicity of operations. However, financial inclusion as a formal banking policy was implemented from 2005 on recommendations of Kamlesh Chandra Chakrabarty committee's report. After this report, the terms and conditions to open bank account by marginalized people were eased by banks.

According to V. Leeladhar, Reserve bank of India bulletin, January 2006, financial inclusion is delivery of banking services at an affordable cost to the vast sections of advantaged and low income groups. Unrestrained access to public goods and services is the *sine qua non* of an open and efficient society. As banking services are in the nature of public good, it is essential that availability of banking and payment services to the entire population without discrimination is the prime objective of the public policy.

According to committee of financial inclusion, "The process of ensuring access to appropriate financial products and services needed by vulnerable groups such as weaker sections and low income groups at an affordable cost in a fair and transparent manner by mainstream Institutional players."

According to M.K.Samantaray, General Manager, Reserve Bank of India, Large segment of population remaining excluded from formal payments system & financial markets when financial market developing & globalizing – Obvious market failure – Government & financial sector regulators creating enabling conditions for inclusive & affordable market.

Rangarajan Committee (2008) on financial inclusion stated that: "Financial inclusion may be defined as the process of ensuring access to financial services and timely and adequate credit where needed by vulnerable groups such as weaker sections and low income groups at an affordable cost." The financial services include the entire gamut of savings, loans, insurance, credit, payments, etc. The financial system is expected to provide its function of transferring resources from surplus to deficit units, but both deficit and surplus units are those with low incomes, poor background, etc. By providing these services, the aim is to help them come out of poverty.

A perusal of literature on finance and economic development reveals that the earlier theories of development concentrated on labor, capital, institutions, etc., as the factors for growth and development. There have been numerous researches analyzing how financial systems help in developing economies. A great deal of consistency exists among economists regarding financial development prompting economic growth. Many theories have established that financial development creates favorable conditions for growth through either a supply leading or a demand-following channel. According to Rajan and Zingales (2003), development of the financial system contributes to economic growth.

Importance of Financial Inclusion in India

A purpose of financial inclusion is to help people and communities meet basic needs such as nutritious food, clean water, housing, education, and healthcare and more by supporting the businesses that provide these services, and enabling clients to have more reliable and affordable access to them. An inclusive financial system is essential infrastructure in every country.

While financial inclusion alone cannot bring people out of poverty, it can help people build better lives. It can help individuals to start businesses, and help small businesses grow into larger ones. Financial services can help small farmers tap into the formal economic system for two-way flow of information and income. Entire economies can grow more quickly and in ways more favorable to poor people.

The policy makers have been focusing on financial inclusion of Indian rural and semi-rural areas primarily for three most important pressing needs:

1. Creating a platform for inculcating the habit to save money – The lower income category has been living under the constant shadow of financial duress mainly because of the absence of savings. The absence of savings makes them a vulnerable lot. Presence of banking services and products aims to provide a critical tool to inculcate the habit to save. Capital formation in the country is also expected to be boosted once financial inclusion measures

materialize, as people move away from traditional modes of parking their savings in land, buildings, bullion, etc.

2. Providing formal credit avenues – So far the unbanked population has been vulnerably dependent of informal channels of credit like family, friends and moneylenders. Availability of adequate and transparent credit from formal banking channels shall allow the entrepreneurial spirit of the masses to increase outputs and prosperity in the countryside. A classic example of what easy and affordable availability of credit can do for the poor is the micro-finance sector.
3. Plug gaps and leaks in public subsidies and welfare programmes – A considerable sum of money that is meant for the poorest of poor do not actually reach them. While this money meanders through large system of government bureaucracy much of it is widely believed to leak and is unable to reach the intended parties. Government is, therefore, pushing for direct cash transfers to beneficiaries through their bank accounts rather than subsidizing products and making cash payments. This laudable effort is expected to reduce government's subsidy bill (as it shall save that part of the subsidy that is leaked) and provide relief only to the real beneficiaries. All these efforts require an efficient and affordable banking system that can reach out to all. Therefore, there has been a push for financial inclusion.

Financial Inclusion is necessary for India mainly due to agrarian nature of Indian economy and her huge population. People belonging to this sector suffer a lot due to high interest rates, uncertain nature of agriculture, absence of sufficient agricultural insurance services, rising production costs and exorbitant amount of interest paid by them to traditional moneylenders. And these are the primary reasons that banking sector is also look upon with suspicion by agriculturists as they have been looking at moneylenders through ages. It was, therefore, important to put a better picture of banking industry before them to break their perceived notions about this sector. Financial inclusion, therefore, was formulated with the main objective of providing basic hassle free financial services such as bank account. Bank accounts are perceived as first important step in providing financial empowerment to the downtrodden and policies of financial inclusion were envisaged keeping in mind the target of brining more and more people under mainstream banking and financial services. Initiatives under financial inclusion have been pressed upon as they are perceived as major tools in achieving sustainable growth.

Finance has come a long way since the time when it wasn't recognized as a factor for growth and development. It is now attributed as the brain of an economic system and most economies strive to make their financial systems more efficient. It also keeps policymakers on their toes as any problem in this sector could freeze the entire economy and even lead to a contagion. The policymakers have set up their task force/committees to understand how financial inclusion can be achieved including advanced economies like United Kingdom.

Conclusion

A series of innovations are making it possible to provide low-cost and convenient financial services to all those who need them. Mobile phones and digital technology are changing how people bank and pay for things, in part by leveraging existing communications infrastructure and retail networks such as stores, airtime agents, post offices, and banks. And financial service institutions are reaching out to clients in new ways, such as through converted trucks with ATMs and tellers that take banking services to remote villages.

Financial products for agriculture, health insurance, and others are inspiring scalable solutions through careful design that meet client needs within their local contexts. Governments are encouraging these and other new models through policies that encourage innovation, partnership, and responsible finance. At the same time, new data efforts are enabling countries and service providers to know more about unbanked markets and client needs, and to measure progress against nationally determined targets.

REVIEW OF LITERATURE

The review of literature is likely to provide bird's eye view of the study conducted on the subject matter. Review of literature is helpful in gaining back ground knowledge of the research topic and identifying the various issue related to it. In this way, it prepares the ground for justification of research plan. Economics growth theory and economics inequalities both provide a starting point for understanding importance for the new path of economic growth policies to sustain the nations. A large numbers of studies have been made so far on financial inclusion in India, yet some gaps still persist. There are still problems of access to finance; credit, poverty and indebtedness have not been adequately examined. Just to open an account in the bank is not the only solution of the problem. Financial literacy is required for the overall achievement of the objective of financial inclusion. The present study is an attempt to find out of regional disparity, indebtedness and status of financial inclusion in India.

After a period of more than sixty years of independence with planned development, several transects are still facing impoverishment in India. Inspire of planner‘s motivation to achieve growth with equality known as “inclusive growth; the country has been facing wide regional disparity between both of urban and rural regions. Poverty, which is a consequence of underdevelopment, is a continuing issue to be tackled with rural indebtedness, has been an agenda of discussion right from the time of independence. Safer, easy and affordable credit and other financial services to the poor and valuable groups, disadvantaged areas and lagging sectors are recognized as preconditions for accelerating growth and reducing income disparities and poverty. Accesses to the financiering of better finance system by creating equal opportunities enables economics and socially excluded people to integrate better into the economy and actively contribute to development and protects themselves against economic shocks (RBI, 2009).

Studies Based on Linkages between Finance and Economic Development

Waiter (1873) and Hicks (1969) argued that finance played a crucial role in ushering in industrialization in England by facilitating mobilization of capital. Schumpeter (1912) contended that well-functioning banks spur technological innovation by identifying and funding potential entrepreneurs. Economists like Robinson (1952) opined that, —where enterprise leads, finance follows‖, thereby taking a positions that economic development create demand for particulars type of financial arrangements and the financial system responds automatically to these demands. Especially, in the context of India, Bell and Rousseau (2001) have shown how financial intermediaries in India have played a leading role in influencing its economic performance. The financial sector, among other things, not only led to promote aggregate investment and output but also to attain finance-led industrialization. Studies by Burgess and Pande (2003) and Burgess et al.(2004) have shown that rural branch expansion in India was associated with non-agricultural growth and has helped in reducing rural poverty. This has been termed by the some as supply leading strategy.

Studies Based on the Inequalities and Economic Growth

Nicoals (1955) reported that in the initial days inequality theories incorrectly stated that inequality had a positive effect on economic development, later it was determined that the marginal tendency to save was to increase with wealth and inequality increases savings and capital accumulation. Therefore, the analysis based on comparing yearly equality figures to yearly growth rates was flawed and misleading because it takes several years for the effects of equality changes to manifest in economic growth changes (Berg & Ostry, 2012).

Rodriguez (2000) studied the relationship between income distribution and economic development which has been subjected to dramatic transformation in the past century. While the Classical economists advanced the hypothesis that inequality is beneficial for economic development, the neoclassical paradigm, which subsequently dominated the field of macroeconomics, dismissed the Classical hypothesis and advanced the viewpoint that the study of income distribution has no significance in the understanding of the growth process.

Atkinson and Audretsch (2008) indicated that innovation was a much effective driver of growth than capital. In the old economy, where large amounts of capital were needed to construct an emergent factory economy, and before the emergence of the kind of sophisticated global capital markets, of today, neoclassic list‘s overriding focus on capital accumulation may have made some sense.

Atkinson (2008) emphasized in his article that Global major economies have been transformed by the forces of technology, globalization, and entrepreneurship and that the doctrines guiding economic policy makers have not kept pace. Robert Atkinson explored innovation economics framework for the 21st century to build a framework for poverty alleviation. In the world, billion poor can be the engine of the next round of global trade and prosperity.

Atkinson (2011) tried to argue that today‘s economy, trying to stimulate the supply of an item that the economy has plenty of investment capital –does not make much sense. The problem in the new economy is not a lack of investment capital but a lack of good investment opportunities. Supply side tax cuts on individuals do not make much difference in the availability of capital; and even if they did, the supply of capital is not the key factor driving economic growth in today's knowledge based economy.

Studies Based on the Economic Growth

Greenwood et al. (1990) tried to introduce two important issues in economic growth theories in a single model. They were relationship between economic growth and inequality, and relation between financial structures and economic growth as it has given a high return on capital. On the other hand economic development has also provided means to financial development.

Kirkpatrick (2000) emphasized on the finance as an essential part for the human development. Financial development was considered to be an integral factor in the economic growth of a country. So far, many studies have noted that a well-functioning financial system, that mobilized savings, allocated resources, and facilitated risk management contributed to economic growth by supporting capital accumulation, improving investment efficiency, and promoting technological innovation.

Beck et al. (2000) tried to evaluate empirically the relationship between level of financial intermediary development and economic growth. They observed a positive impact of financial intermediary development on the growth of total factor productivity which would lead to economic development institutional agencies.

Calderon and Liu (2003) used data on 109 developing and developed countries – and showed that the direction of causality was generally from financial development to economic growth. Moreover, economic growth is likely to be beneficial to the poorest segment of the population, as indicated by the result of a study by Becket et al. (2007). They used data from a sample of 72 developed and developing countries for the period 1960-2005 and found a positive relationship between financial depth [as measured by the ratio of private sector credit to gross domestic product (GDP)] and the change in the share of the lowest quintile in total national personal income.

Bekaert et al. (2004) examined a positive impact of equity market liberalization on real economic growth. Further, they also observed the positive impact of capital account liberalization and quality of financial institutions on economic growth.

World Bank (2008) proposed Economic Growth Theories of development advocating that financial development created enabling condition for growth through either a "supply-leading" (financial development spurs growth) or a "demand-following" (growth generates demand for financial products) channel. Earlier theory of development hypothesized that rise in inequality was inevitable in the early stages of development. The earlier literature did not focus on the need to develop an extensive financial system that could tap saving and then channel the funds so generated to a wide spectrum of activities. The modern development theory perceived the lack of access to financial as a critical factor responsible for persistent income inequality as well as slower growth. A large body of improving access to fiancé might accelerate economic growth along with a reduction in income inequality and poverty. Without an inclusive financial system, poor individual and small enterprises had to rely on their own limited savings and earnings to invest in their education and entrepreneurship to take advantage of growth opportunities.

Blackemore and Herrendorf (2009) concluded in their report that Economic growth is critically important for individual well-being. Specifically, even small differences in growth rates over long horizons led to large differences in living standard. Economists learned a great deal about growth and development and a consensus was forming.

Studies Based on the Concept of Financial Inclusion

Sharma and Pais (2008) analyzed the Indian history with the concept of financial inclusion started in the year of 1904 as cooperative movement, and then it gained momentum in 1969, when 14 major commercial banks of the countries were nationalized and lead bank scheme was introduced shortly thereafter from that year the majority of bank branches were opened in large number across the country and even in the areas which were hitherto being neglected. However, there was severe gap in financial assessment which needed special attention. Many studies have proved that lack of inclusion was rather exclusion from the banking system which resulted in a loss of 1 percent to the GDP. Thus, the Reserve Bank of India concluded that the financial inclusion was not just a socio-political imperative but also an economic one and realized the gravity of the problem. Finally, the Reserve Bank of India made the Mid Term Review of Monetary Policy (2005-06), urged the banks to make financial inclusion as one of their prime objectives.

Suryanarayan (2008) proposed to define inclusion/exclusion with reference to an outcome scenario for broad-based growth as reflected in estimates of production, income, and consumption distribution. This should facilitate a sketch of occupational, social, regional profiles of the excluded in the mainstream growth process. This study, therefore, made an attempt to provide a perspective, a measure of inclusion, and finally an evaluation based on the available estimates of consumption distribution for the year 2004-05 for India.

Hanning and Jansen (2010) found that reliable and comprehensive data capturing various dimensions of financial inclusion was a critical condition for evidence-based Policymaking. This presented several challenges ranging from the basics of what financial inclusion was and what it entailed especially because it was a concept that varied with level of countries' economic development and geographical reasons. The definition of financial inclusion and its components was important for setting a clear direction for policymaking by translating the concept of financial inclusion into operational terms but also allowing tracking progress and measuring outcomes of policy reforms. This study attempted to articulate the definition of financial inclusion and its components in the context of Kenya.

Singh (2012) discussed that as the poverty level declined and households have greater levels of discretionary incomes, they would be first time financial servers. They would, therefore, need to have easy access to formal financial systems to get into the banking habit. Banks would need to innovate and devised newer methods of including such customers into their fold. Innovation in the form of business facilitators and correspondents would be needed for banks to increase their outreach for bank to ensure financial inclusion. He emphasized the financial inclusion as a great step to alleviate poverty in India. But to achieve this, the government should provide a less perspective environment in which banks were free to pursue the innovations necessary to reach low income consumers and still make a profit. Financial service providers should learn more about the consumers and new business models to reach them. New entrants to the banking, system need household at their doorstep. There has been a burst of entrepreneurship across the country, spanning rural, and semi-urban and urban areas. This has to be nurtured and financed. It was only through growth of enterprises across all size and that competition would be fostered. With the increasing liberalization and higher economic growth, the role of the banking sector was poised to increase in the financing pattern of economic activities within the country. Financial inclusion would strengthen financial depending and provide resources to the banks to expand credit delivery. He concluded that financial inclusion would lead to financial development in our country which will in turn help to accelerate economic growth.

Aggarwal (2012) made an attempt to understand the financial inclusion from the behavioural perspective both on supply and demand end. There were risks and return associated with every transaction that we needed to quantified but certain behavioural motives failed the implementation of economics but can be as marketing proposition to gain high level of inclusion. The study was based on the personal interaction and opinion survey. This evaluation from the behavioural perspective provided the scope for the policy-makers and marketers to strategically align their approach with the behavioural aspect, without confining their thoughts to the economical evaluations.

Studies Based on the Definition of Financial Inclusion

Institution

Author Definition

Indicators

ADB (2000)

Provision of a board range of financial services such as deposits, loan, payment services, money transfers and insurance to poor and low income households and their micro-enterprises.

Deposits, loans,

payment services,

Money transfer and insurance.

Stephen P. Sinclair (2001)

Financial exclusion means the inability to access necessary financial services in an appropriate form. Exclusion can come about as a result of problems with access, conditions, prices, marketing, or self exclusion in response to negative experiences or perceptions.

Basic banking services for money transmission, credit, and insurance, debt and debt assistance, long –term savings and financial literacy.

Chant Link and Associates,

Australia (2004)

Financial exclusion is back of access by certain consumers to appropriate low cost, fair, and safe financial products and services from mainstream providers. Financial exclusion becomes a concern in the community when it applies to lower income consumers and/or those in financial hardship.

Deposit accounts, direct investments, home loans, credit cards, personal loan, building insurance and home insurance.

Treasury Committee, House of Commons UK (2004)

Ability of individuals to access appropriate financial products and services.

Affordable credit and savings for all and access to financial advice.

Scottish Government (2005)

Access for individuals to appropriate financial products and services. This includes have the capacity, skills, knowledge and understanding to make the best use of those products and services. Financial exclusion by contrast, is the converse of this.

Access to products and services, and/or capacity, skills, knowledge and understanding.

United Nations (2006)

A financial sector that provides 'access' to credit for all 'bankable' people and firms, to insurance for all insurable people and firms and to savings and payments services for everyone. Inclusive finance does not require that everyone who is eligible use each of the services, but they should be able to choose to use them if desired.

Access to credit, insurance, savings, payment services.

Report of the Committee on

Financial Inclusion in India Chairman: C. Rangarajan, (2008)

The process of insuring access to financial services and timely and adequate credit where needed by vulnerable groups such as weaker sections and low income groups at an affordable cost.

Access to financial services and timely and adequate credit.

Word Bank (2008)

Board access to financial services implies an absence of price and non-price barriers in the use of financial services; it is difficult to define and measure because access has many dimensions.

Access to financial services such as deposit, credit, payments, insurance.

Treasury (2004) concluded that particularly those living on low income, could not access mainstream financial products such as bank accounts and low cost loans, which, in turn, imposed real costs on them, often the most vulnerable people in urban and rural India.

Meadows et al. (2004) argued that the focus narrowed down mainly to the products and services provided by the mainstream financial services providers. But just providing the services for poor is different from the actual need to design particular products or services at the affordable cost-effective products.

United Nations (2006) defined financial inclusion as the timely delivery of financial services to disadvantaged sections of society. But this definition encompassed concept's primary dimension. Firstly, financial inclusion referred to a customer access to a range of formal financial services, from simple credit and saving services to the more complex such as insurance and pensions. Secondly, financial inclusion implied that customers have access to more than one financial services provider, which ensured a variety of competitive options. Following from this definition, financial exclusion would mean the inability of the disadvantaged to access financial services. A range of obstacle could lead to financial exclusion; barriers including geography (limiting physical access), regulations (lack of formal identification proof or of appropriate products and poor households), psychology (fear of financial institution's staff, structures, complicated financial products, etc.), information (lack of knowledge regarding products and procedures), and low financial acumen (low income and poor financial discipline), among others.

World Bank (2008) reported that access to financial service implied an absence of obstacles to the use of these services, even though there were some obstacles as price or non-price barrier to finances. The majority of the developing countries had failed to make this distinction could complicate effort to define and measure access. Financial market imperfections, such as information asymmetries and transaction cost, were likely to be especially binding on the talented poor and on micro and small enterprises that lack collateral, credit histories, and connections. Without inclusive financial systems, these individuals and enterprises with promises opportunities were limited to their own savings.

Studies Based on the Financial Exclusion

Kempson et al. (2000) analyzed the range of physical and geographical barriers to financial inclusive factor that can contribute to financial exclusive for different products and individuals under certain circumstances. There are a number of 'dimensions' or 'forms' of financial exclusion that have been identified. The critical dimension of financial exclusion include: (i) access exclusion –restriction of access through the process of risk management (by financial services providers); (ii) condition exclusion –conditions attached to financial products which make them inappropriate for the needs of some segments of population; (iii) price exclusion some people can only gain access to financial products at prices they cannot afford; (iv) marketing exclusion –some people are effectively excluded by targeted marketing and sales; and (v) self exclusive –people decide not to opt for financial product of the fear of refusal access by the services providers. However, in many countries, many non-poor individuals, micro, small and medium entrepreneurs also have difficulty in accessing financial services.

Sinclair (2001) indicated that the nature and forms of exclusion and the factors responsible for it are varied for it is varied and, thus, no single factor could explain the phenomenon. So the principal barriers in the expansion of financial services are often indentified as physical access, high charges, and penalties, conditions attached to products which make them inappropriate or complicated and perceptions of financial service institutions which are thought to be unwelcoming to low income people.

Reserve Bank of India (2008) emphasized that the Financial Exclusion was broadly defined as the lack of access by certain segments of the society (SC, ST, OBC, and women) to suitable, low-cost, fair, and safe financial products and services from mainstream providers‖. Thus the essence of financial inclusion was to insure that a range of appropriate financial services was available at affordable price to every individual and access those services. In reality, the reserve bank of India found that the main reasons for financial exclusion, from the demand side are lack of awareness, low income, poverty and illiteracy; and from the supply side it was the distance from branch, branch timings, cumbersome documentation and procedures, unsuitable products, language, staff attitudes, etc. The RBI found that due to all these procedural hassles people felt it easier to take money from informal credit sources, in spite of high cost of credit. It resulted in compromised standard of living and higher costs. Informal credit increased exposure to unethical and unregulated providers and vulnerability to uninsured risks. The RBI concluded that financial inclusion did not mean merely opening of saving bank account but signified creation of awareness about the financial products, education, and advised on money management, offering debt counseling, and etc. by banks. Every society should ensure easy access to public goods. Therefore, banking service being a public good should also be aimed at providing service to the entire population.

Sharma (2010) distinguished between five factor that account for the lack of financial inclusion (exclusion): (1) Access exclusion due to geography and "risk management of financial system", (2) Condition exclusion "due to conditions that are inappropriate for some people" (3) Price exclusion due to non affordability of financial services, (4) Marketing exclusion due to the non attractiveness of conducting business with certain groups within society (lending risk), and (5) Self exclusion, due to "fear of refusal due to psychological barriers".

Studies Based on the Global Financial Exclusion

Kempson (2006) showed that in Sweden lower than two percent of adults did not have an account in 2000 and in Germany, the figure was around three percent. Another research by (Buckland et al (2005) showed that less than four percent of adults in Canada and five percent in Belgium, lacked a bank account. Therefore, it is also mentioned in academia that a better way to analyze financial inclusion in developing economies is to actually see financial exclusion.

World Bank (2010) reported that in the largest share of the unbanked live in Sub-Saharan Africa (12 percent banked) and South Asia (24 percent banked), East Asia, Middle East and North Africa, Latin America and Eastern Europe and Central Asia are also low-access regions with less than 50 percent of their population banked. Among the unbanked a large proportion survived on less than $5 dollars a day. Finally the report concluded that financial inclusion needs to leverage all financial services providers, for example micro-finance industry as well as from recent innovations to deliver financial service outside of conventional bank branches. However, filling the financial service gap would require significant commitment from a wide variety of bank and non-bank financial institution, including commercial bank, credit unions, savings banks, microfinance institutions, postal banks, and mobile banking operators.

Diniz et al. (2011) presented an interesting case study of how the 'banked people' (i.e., people having a checking or saving account) of Autazes (an Amazon county) found it extremely expensive and time consuming to use their bank facilities before 2002 when banking facilities were not locally available. This study was a peculiar case where the people of Autazes were financially included while Autazes, as a region itself, was financial inclusion that only counts number of people having a bank account will not reflect the lack of adequate financial services as in the case of Autazes before 2002. Further, adequate utilization of financial service was also an important aspect of financial inclusion.

Studies Based on the Structural Disclamation of Exclusion in India

The extent of exclusion was pointed out as under during the 59th round of NSSO Survey:

(a) General

- The majority of farmer households, 51.4 percent, were financially excluded from both formal and informal sources.
- The total farmer households, only 27 percent, access formal sources, but one third of this group also borrowed from non-formal sources.
- Overall 73 percent of farmer households had no access to formal sources of credit.
- Exclusion was most acute in Central; Eastern and North-Eastern regions have a concentration of 64 percent of all financially excluded farmer households in the country.
- Overall indebtedness to formal sources of finance alone was only 19.66 percent in these three regions.

(b) Occupational Groups

- Marginal farmer households constituted 66 percent of total farmer households. Only 45 percent of these households were indebted to either formal or non formal sources of finance.
- Only 20 percent of indebted marginal farmer households had access to formal sources of credit.
- The majority 80 percent of the non-cultivator households had not accessed credit from any source.

(c) Social Groups

- The majority 36 of ST Farmer households were indebted (SCs and Other Backward Classes –OBC -51%) mostly to informal sources.
- Analysis of the data provided by RBI through its Basic Statistical Returns revealed that critical exclusion (in terms of credit) was manifest in 256 districts, spread across 17 State and 1 UT, with a credit gap of 95 percent and above. This was in respect of commercial banks and RRBs.

Studies Based on the Present Scenario of Financial Exclusion in India

Roy (2012) emphasized that out of 6, 00,000 habitations in the country; only about 5 percent had a commercial bank branch. Also only about 57 percent of the population across the country had bank account (savings), and this ratio was much lower in the North-Eastern states. Further, 13 percent of the population had debit cards and 2 percent had credit cards. India had a significantly low level of financial penetration compared with OECD countries. In India, access to finance access to credit was worse off when compared with China, Malaysia, and Thailand. However, in terms of financial access through ATMs for rural population, India fared poorly compared to select Asian peer group countries (RBI, 2010).

Khan (2012) indicated that the Habitation in the country which has a commercial bank branch is: 30,000 (out of 600,000).

The above table provides a set of summary statistics relating to penetration of various categories of financial products. First, the relatively low penetration of bank branches must be highlighted – only 30,000 out of 6, 00,000 habitations have a banking presence. As is well understood, the goal of having physical banking facility in every habitation is unrealistic, which is why the inclusion strategy is largely based on the use of Information and communication technology (ICT) to expand banking access virtually through the mechanism of a Business Correspondent (BC), who carries a handheld device networked to the bank systems. This is enormous technological discontinuity enabled by the spread and efficiency of the mobile telephone network and, clearly, the inclusion strategy must take full advantage of this resource.

Studies Based on the Financially Excluded Groups

FATF (2011) emphasized that disadvantaged and other vulnerable groups such as SC, ST and Women, including low income households, handicapped, individuals in rural communities and undocumented migrants, in both developed and developing jurisdictions, were more likely to be excluded from the formal, regulated financial sector, because of other barriers such as problems in meeting the documentary and other requirements, non-awareness, wrong perceptions, limited knowledge, high cost, etc. Underserved clients represent a very heterogeneous category with very different risk profiles in different jurisdictions. As a consequence, they could not be classified as low risk clients on the sole basis that they were financially excluded.

Studies Based on the Consequences of Financial Exclusion

RBI (2008) explained the long history of sound banking system developed by RBI after Independence, which could support planned economic development through mobilization of resource/deposits and channel them into productive sectors. Hence, In order to overcome the exclusion RBI wanted to expand the credit and financial services to the wider sections of the population and a wide network of financial institutions had been established over the years. The organized financial system comprising commercial banks, regional rural banks (RRBs), urban co-operative bank (UCBs), primary agricultural credit societies (PACS), and post offices catered to needs of the financial services of the people besides MFIs, self help group. Furthermore, development of the institutional framework during that period had focused on new strategies of expanding financial service involving credit dispensation using multiple channels such as civil society organizations (NGOs), post offices, farmers' clubs, and panchayats as business facilitators/correspondents. Specific financial instruments/products were also developed in order to promote financial inclusion.

However, the RBI had taken various initiatives that could broadly be categorized into three phases. The first phase was started in the late year of 1960s through the 1980s. In this year the main focus was on gateway of credit to the neglected sectors of the economy. So, the RBI emphasized on weaker sections of the society. In the year 1990 second phase was started through March 2005. The RBI had focused mainly on strengthening the financial institutions as part of financial sector reforms. In this phase financial inclusion was encouraged mainly by introducing SHG-bank linkage programme and Kisan Credit Cards (KCCs) for providing credit to farmers. The final phase was beginning in April 2005. In this phase "financial inclusion" was explicitly made as a major policy objective and trust was on providing safe facility of savings deposits through "no frills" accounts.

Agrawal (2011) indicated that financial exclusive was a serious concern among SC, ST, OBC and women households as well as small businesses, mainly located in semi-urban and rural areas. The main consequences of financial exclusion being financial excluded the absence of access to bank accounts and other saving opportunities result in lack of savings, low investments and lack of financial planning, then it became difficult in gaining access to credit getting credit for informal sources at exorbitant rates resulted in increased unemployment due to lack of self-employment opportunities as well as higher incidence of crime etc. Therefore, small business might suffer due to loss of access to middle class, and higher-income consumers, higher cash handling costs, delays in remittances of money, lots of reliance on private money lenders for small credits. He concluded that financial exclusion not only widens the "Rich-Poor divide", it also led to "Social Exclusion".

Studies Based on the Status of Financial Inclusion in India

Pahuja (2007) analyzed the historical and the then state of the rural financial system in India. The study was divided into three major segments where Segment (1) presented the background of the rural financial system and also studied the problem of financial exclusion, segment (II) dealt with the institutions working for the rural financial system, segment (III) focused on Micro Finance Institutions and deals with the analysis of the overall paradigm as it hold for the Micro Finance Institutions in India.

Noman (2013) conducted a district level study on the model of Financial Inclusion Index (FII) between 2007 and 2010 to analyze the changes of FII in Bangladesh. Though FII ranking of 19 districts had shown positive changes but ranking of 10 districts had not shown changes where 35 districts had negatively changed among the 64 districts of Bangladesh. Some of the reasons of slow financial information, and high account maintenance balance were low income of people and high cost of banking product. This study shown the status, problems and key points of financial inclusion in Bangladesh by using three dimensions of financial inclusion to measure the FII value which indicated the coverage, availability, input and output of banking services to compute the status, level and magnitude of financial inclusion in division/district of Bangladesh and to give a better idea for making fruitful decision to ensure stable and equitable economic growth of the country.

Sahu (2013) reviewed the status of India's financial inclusion, to estimate the financial inclusion index for various states in India and to study the relationship between financial inclusion Index and Social-economic Variables. It was found that no state in India was belonging to high IFI group. Two states namely; Chandigarh and Delhi were belonging to medium IFI, and rests of the states had low IFI values. The coefficient of PNSDP was positively associated with financial inclusion. Regression results revealed that 34 percent of the change in financial inclusion was explained by per capita net state domestic product. In a country like India with diverse social and economic profile, financial education was particularly relevant for people who were poor and who operated at the margin and were vulnerable to persistent downward financial pressures. Banks should be asked to take up financial inclusion as a business opportunity to help the poor come under the banking operation net.

Arulmuran et al. (2013) reviewed the current status of financial inclusion in India and the world in general and highlighting the measures taken by the Govt. of India and RBI for promoting financial inclusion and the inter-linkage between social-economic welfare and financial inclusion. During last 40 years huge infrastructure that has penetrated even remote rural areas has been able to serve only a small part of the potential customers. In order to achieve the goal of total financial inclusion, policy makers, MFI, NGOs and regulators have to work together.

Studies Based on the Efforts Made for Financial Inclusion in Past

Leeladhar (2005) observed that despite making significant improvements in all areas relating to financial viability, profitability and competitiveness, there were concerns that banks had not able to include vast segment of the population, especially the underprivileged sections of the society, into the fold of basic banking services.

However, in 2003, the RBI policy of financial inclusion was to provide access to financial service to the poor could be earmarked as another bold initiative in serving the rural transects targeting inclusive growth. Committee on financial inclusion in 2008 (Rangarajan Committee) observed that financial inclusion to hitherto excluded segments of the population was critical to sustain and accelerate growth momentum. For achievement of the same, the committee had put forward multi-pronged strategies include establishment of National mission on financial inclusion, revitalizing the RRBs and Cooperatives, introducing MFI model (SHG-bank linkage) and Business Facilitator and Business Correspondents Model.

Studies Based on the Role of Banks in Financial Inclusion

Gundannavar (1992) highlighted the role of banks in implementing social banking schemes to keep pace with changing social needs. He strongly opposed any move to reduce resources allocation to priority sectors, which would have an adverse impact on the agricultural credit. He suggested increasing higher interest rate on commercial lending and to continue concessional rate of lending to priority sectors.

Burgess and Pande (2005) studied the effect of the rural bank branch expansion which took place in India during the period 1977 to 1990, as a result of specific rule. The rule was that a bank could open a branch in an area with other existing bank branches, only if it also opened branches in four other areas with no bank branches. It was found that there was a significant fall in rural poverty and there was an increase and increase in nonagricultural output.

Anand and Saxena (2012) focused on all the initiatives taken so far by the Indian commercial banks in terms of technology, distribution channels and initiatives for financial education for the unbanked masses. Initiatives analyzed would actually benefit to those banks that had not yet implemented any of the initiatives, and would also be beneficial to the general public to make them aware about the steps which were being taken for them and to spread out the reach of the banks to the unbanked masses. This study was based on exploratory study in which secondary data was used for collecting information. They concluded that banks needed to redesign their business strategies to incorporate specific plans to promote financial inclusion of low income group treating it both at business opportunities as well as a corporate social responsibility.

Pal and Pal (2012) analyzed in their study the income related inequality in financial inclusion in India using a representative household level survey data, linked to State-level factors. This study also provided estimates of the effect of various socio, economic and demographic characteristics of households on propensity of a household to use formal financial services, and compare that for rural and urban sectors. A notable result was that greater availability of banking services fosters financial inclusion, particularly among the poor.

Mukherjee and Chakraborty (2012) critically examined and highlighted the role and efficiency of the commercial banks doing business in the state of Jharhand in connection with their responsibility towards promoting financial inclusion. The study also aimed at examining the capacity and role of institutions like regional rural banks (RRBs), self help groups (SHGs), non-banking financial companies (NBFCs) for the purpose of promoting financial inclusion in the state.

Mukherjee & Chakraborty (2012) reviewed the primary responsibility of ensuring financial inclusion lies with the Central Bank (RBI). However, due to the huge size and diversity of population the commercial banks have been taking the assistance of various social and financial entities like co-operative banks, regional rural banks (RRBs), selfhelp groups (SHGs), joint liability groups, and other non-banking finance companies. The objective was critically examined and highlighted the role and efficacy of the commercial banks doing business in the state of Jharkhand in connection with their responsibility towards promoting financial inclusion. The study also aimed at examining the capacity and role of other institutions mentioned above for the purpose of promoting financial inclusion in the state. They suggested that every bank, be it in the public sector or private sector, reports to the RBI on its achievement on financial inclusion more frequently as a statutory requirement.

Shroff and Prasadarao (2012) studied the financial inclusion Initiatives undertaken by Reserve Bank of India/ NABARD/Government of India, etc. Primary data collection was through questionnaire, face to face meeting in order to study the issue of financial inclusion in the select village and from the findings for the data collected – analyzed the same and suggested BCs/BFs Model from implementation by Banks. They remarked that to sum up, banks need to redesign their business strategies to incorporate specific plans to promote financial inclusion of low income group treating it both a business opportunity as well as a corporate social responsibility.

Kuppan (2012) found that the main reason for financial exclusion was lack of regular or substantial income. He found that in most of the cases people with low income did not qualify for a loan. The proximity of the financial service was another fact. The loss was not only the transportation cost but also the loss of daily wages for a low income individual. Most of excluded consumers were not aware of bank products, which were beneficial for them. Getting money for their financial requirement from a local money leader was easier than getting loan from the bank. Most of the banks required collateral for their loans. It was very difficult for a low income individual to find collateral for the bank loan. Moreover, banks gave more importance to meeting their financial targets. So they focused on larger accounts. It was not profitable for banks to provide small loan and make a profit. Financial inclusion was a great step to alleviate poverty in India. But to achieve this, the government should provide a less perspective environment in which banks are free to pursue the innovation necessary to reach low income consumer and still make a profit. Financial service providers should learn more about the consumers and new business models for them.

Thapar (2013) tried to study the financial inclusion programmes in the selected bank branches within Ludhiana districts in Punjab (India) and to find out the steps taken by the banks in the area of financial inclusion. The study concluded that though the banks were complying with RBI norms but still a lot of efforts were to be put in for financial inclusion progress.

Studies Based on the Credit

Ansari (2007) revealed that reaching the poorest, whose credit requirements were very small, frequent and unpredictable, was found to be difficult. Further, the emphasis was on providing credit rather than financial products and services including savings, insurance, etc. to the poor to meet their simple requirements. Therefore, need was felt for alternative policies, systems and procedures, savings and loans products, other complementary services and new delivery mechanisms, which would fulfill the requirements of the poorest.

Rath (2008) expressed his concern on farmer‘s suicide and debt burden by various reasons influencing the life of the poor in this study. Poor farmer‘s death due to the unbearable burden of debt was the matter of concern. It highlighted how loan waiver would lighten the burden of the farmer though. In the long run, it adversely affected the rural credit institutions that extended loans to farmers. Since the bulk of the loans would be from outside institutions, there was a strong possibility of the demand for writing off loans in times to come.

Bhattacharjee et al. (2009) conducted a study of the informal Credit in West Bengal addressing two important issues relating to credit market in developing countries i.e., household‘s accessibility was concerned it was observed that the urban poor faced grater problems accessing credit. The receiving fewer loan from both formal and informal lending credit markets. Further, analysis of interest rate formation in credit markets and found that the developed districts of West Bengal (WB) are characterized by the presence of less formal lending (by total number of loan outstanding), accompanied by a higher probability of exorbitant interest rates in market of professional money lenders. Thus, there was excess demand for credit in the developed districts of West Bengal. It was also observed that the professional and non-professional moneylenders (as a result of having less information about borrowers) faced higher risks of default charge and thus charged higher rate of interest.

Sriharsha (2011) studied the flow of credit to small borrowers with the objective to evaluate the extent of financial inclusion based on credit to small borrowers with special reference to agricultural credit in Andhra Pradesh. This study attempted to fill this gap by evaluating the extent of financial inclusion in Andhra Pradesh based on the penetration of credit to small borrowers.

Bhavani and Bhanumurthy (2012) pointed out the access to financial service in the agriculture sector enables farmers to financial short-run input costs, long-run investments, and to take care of production uncertainties due to weather and/or other factors. They found financial access enabled micro and small enterprises to have the financial resources required for running their operations. In addition to this, access to financial services such as savings, credit, payments and insurance are necessary conditions in the modern times of increasing leverage of finance for the individuals/households to manage themselves and to explore available opportunities to improve their economic position further.

Dutt and Samanta (2012) conducted a study on the livelihood of people on the chars of the Damondar River in deltaic Bengal in eastern India. Different phases of this self funded intensive field-based empirical research were carried out from 2002 to 2010. This paper explores the multiple sources of informal credit that poor have created. Investigates how these sources are mobilized and accessed by individuals, and highlights the role of informal credit in livelihoods and the overall well-being of individuals, households and communities. The poor often have more faith in moneylenders than they do in banks, especially as they need quick access to money. They also value personal relationships which often help them to survive through extreme crisis. The diversified livelihood base developed through social relationships should not be beyond understanding of policymakers who need to think about ways a bottom up approach can be developed to understand what poor people do, what they need and when they need it to sustain their livelihoods. They found that before we connect the poor to the mainstream financial systems through Bank Linkage or other policy instruments, it was also required to look at the specific contexts in which the poor lived and managed money ingenuously through informal networks. Such as the need to marry off daughters comprise a significant reason for running into debt. The first household illustrated this and suggested that just financial inclusion. The implication of the study was that policy interventions that aimed to tag the poor to the bottom rung of the formal monetary system as micro partners need rethinking.

Shankaraiah and Kumar (2012) conducted a study on rural credit in Andhra Pradesh assessing the performance of financial institutions. They thoroughly discussed the repayment performance of the borrowers and suggested measures for the recovery of over dues from the borrowers.

Lakshmi and Visalakshmi (2013) reviewed that there was lack of assessment of the extent of financial inclusion based on credit flow to small borrowers in Indian economy. The liberalized, increasingly global, market driven economy of India today, has failed to facilitate inclusion and emphasized the active participation of Co-operatives as important tools of financial inclusion in India.

Studies Based on the Saving

Murdoch and Aghion (2005) argued that the poor had no savings because the desire to borrow (to consume) was greater than the desire to save. It might be the case, but many studies shown that the poor actually had a high marginal propensity to save. The fact that microfinance was inherently risky could not be discounted because of the target clientele; there existed risk of borrower payment default. It was, however, observed that microfinance institutions had good repayment rates in the past few years because of the structure of microfinance itself. With the employment of group lending that highly imposed personal collection effort as well as social pressure as collateral loan port folio risk was minimized.

Ramasubbian and Duraiswamy (2012) suggested in their study that though over the past six years the Financial Inclusion strategy had improved the life style of BPL, but missing focus on savings and credit improvement strategies degrades the benefit of financial inclusion. This study analyzed the issues pertaining to implementation of financial inclusion in economically down trodden districts of Tamil Nadu (India). SPSS (SPSS 2011) was used to analyze the data collected from the districts.

Studies Based on the Financial Literacy Programmes

Dutta & Dutta (2011) reviewed the effect on literacy percentage and branch density on financial inclusion in 35 states on union territories in India. They used quintile regression to evaluate the significance of the impact of these two factors. The data on adult population (above 19 years) and literacy percentage for each state/union territory was obtained from 2001 Census report. Data on the number of bank offices and total number of deposit (saving/current/term deposit) account for each state/union territory were obtained from the Reserve Bank of India and BSR Report 2009. They concluded that branch density in a state measured the opportunity for financial inclusion in that state. Literacy was observed as a prerequisite for creating investment awareness, and hence intuitively it seemed to be a key tool for financial inclusion. But the above observations also implied that literacy alone could not guarantee high level financial inclusion in a state. Branch density had a significant impact on financial inclusion. It was not possible to achieve financial inclusion only by creating investment awareness, without significantly improving the investment opportunities in a state. It was observed that if a state/union territory was among the top 20 percent in terms of financial inclusion, with a given level of literacy, then increase in literacy percentage could further improve the level of financial inclusion in that region.

Nalini (2011) reviewed that financial literacy was a primary step for financial inclusion which made people seek and receive financial services and promote the financial literacy among micro, small and medium enterprises by relaxing procedures and establishing customer care.

Studies Based on the Self Help Group Programmes

Rangappa et al. (2008) shown that the self help group (SHG) bank linkage programmes had increased the flow of institutions credit to households and discourages non institutional borrowing through the thrift creation. The study was based on the primary data collected in Davangere district of Karnataka State. Though the district was being served by 87 branches of commercial bank and 42 branches of regional rural banks besides a large number of credit cooperative societies financial inclusion continued to be a major challenge. In this study arithmetic mean values of borrowing during 1-7-2006 to 1-6-2007 from institutional and non-institutional sources were computed separately for the households 'without SHG' and households 'with SHG'. Results of this study were clear that the SHG-Bank linkage programmes had increased the flow of institutional credit to landless and marginal farm households and discouraged no-institutional borrowing through the thrift creation.

Sarma and Pais (2010) reported that literacy was positively and significantly associated with financial inclusion. Several empirical studies (Adhikary and Bagli, 2010, 2011) conducted in West Bengal have shown that SHGs created a smooth path of financial inclusion for the rural poor. The number of total deposit accounts had increased to 734.8 million and credit account to 118.6 million in 2010 for all banks and the number of no-frill accounts in all public and private banks had increased to 33 million in 2009 from seven million in 2006 (RBI, 2010). Besides, KCC scheme had brought 95 million farmers under the purview of the banking system in 2010 as against 84.6 million farmers in 2009 and the SHG bank linkage programme had helped seven million rural people to have access to formal savings and formal credit (Government of India, 2011).

Badgar (2012) revealed that more than 65 percent of the Indian population was still 'unbanked' and did not have access to basic banking facilities. As a mission to sustain the economic development of the country it is imperative that these people be brought, initially, into the banking fold, which subsequently could act as a base for providing other services? The movement of financial inclusion had been one of the real hopes for inclusive growth. The poor and the excluded have successfully organized themselves in 25 lakh self help group (SHGs). With the phenomenal growth recorded by microfinance in recent year-62 percent p.a. in terms of number of unique clients and 88 percent p.a. in terms of portfolio over the past five years and around 27 million borrowers accounts, the SHG linkage programmes had achieved a phenomenal growth over the years but there was still a larger segment of society that was denied access to financial services. SKS Microfinance Ltd., India.

Maiti et al. (2012) pointed out that there were number of traditional and informal ways of forwarding credit before the emergence of the SHGs. All of them provided very little attention to the question of both empowerment and sustainability. Along with this there was a casual approach towards the accountability of the credits leading to adverse impact on both repayments as well as further outreach. The conclusion that emerged from this study was that SHGs were playing a vital role in the rural empowerment, although most of SHSs were formed as a female group.

Uma and Rupa (2013) highlighted the role of SHGs in financial inclusion. The primary data was collected through random sampling method and reflected the positive relationship between SHGs membership and financial inclusion. The study shown after the membership to SHGs there was increase in the number of bank accounts by members to the extent of 82.7 percent from 17.3 percent before membership. The credit availed by the members and annual repayment of the loan also shown positive trend. SHGs helped the deprived section of the people to enter into formal financial sector and given boost to social and economic empowerment.

Studies Based on the Micro Finance

Ghosh (2007) examined the role of microfinance in improving the financial inclusion vulnerable groups of the society such as marginalized farmers, low income group etc. The study used the time series data from 1991 to 2007 on selected variables like bank branches, financially excluded population and impact of SHGs linkages programmed with banks. Data were obtained from various sources such as Hand Book of Statistics on Indian Economy, Reserve Bank of India and Economic Survey. Banks (POSBs), SHGs and microfinance could be used to cater the financial needs of rural India.

Kumar and Saxena (2011) reviewed that microfinance was being pursued through self helping group-bank linkage model and microfinance institutions. The broad objective of policy innovations was to enlarge its coverage and ensured provisions of timely and adequate credit at reasonable rate of interest to a large segment of population as possible. They studied the extent of financial inclusion in India through microfinance enlightened the areas to be worked upon and discussed the required means for people empowerment and financial inclusion.

Badar (2012) pointed out that microfinance was a promising alternative which offers funds at the door steps of the poor and weaker section of the population in rural areas. For this system to operate upon, it had to have very low defaults. The success of microfinance was based upon local mechanism that offered a great deal of flexibility that allowed for lending decisions based on knowledge about specific individuals. What immediately required was to strengthen the voice of borrowers and curb that of national and global capital? As the global recession had hit investment potential and opportunities elsewhere in the world, lending to Indian poor population could be extremely attractive option for private firms from the developed economics.

Choudhary (2013) reviewed the various issues which had been addressed in the literature of microfinance. Data deficiency and non-availability of reliable literature had been a major constraint in the pursuance of this study. An attempt had been made to examine the microfinance institutions and the self help group's role in examining the case of scheduled tribes in the districts of Hoshangabad, Shore & Raisen (Madhya Pardesh). Efforts had also been directed towards suggesting some effective practical measures for alleviating the conditions of this major section of the society. Both primary & secondary data was used in the study to perform the research. The study had followed both qualitative and quantitative methods. She concluded that microfinance services would surely lead to achieve the motive of poverty reduction. Efforts were required to spread awareness among people regarding the microfinance services available and their uses.

Shanker (2013) analyzed the microfinance institutions (MFI) adequately breaking down the barriers of financial services access in India. Two lines of enquiry were followed: the spread of microfinance penetration in the country was analyzed and field interviews of 103 MFI field officers were conducted. It was found that while MFIs broke down many barriers to financial inclusion, there were limitations in the extent of their outreach to those excluded. First, MFI penetration in the country was skewed and excluded some areas neglected the banking sector, suggesting a need for policy incentives to encourage expansion to those areas even in areas in which MFIs operated they were able to provide services to some financially excluded individuals on account of their methods of operation. To provide greater and more lasting access to more individuals there was a need for MFI to consider adopting more flexible operating models and to offer portability of accounts. The study found that microfinance penetration in the country was known uniform with state specifics factors playing a major role in micro finance growth while MFI broke down many barriers to financial inclusion there were limitations in that MFI penetration in the country skewed and excluded some areas neglected by the banking sector suggesting a need for policy incentives.

Studies Based on the Inclusive Growth

World Bank (2008) reported that access to financial service implied an absence of obstacles to the use of these services, even though there were some difficult obstacles is price or non-price barrier to finances. The majority of the developing countries, failed to make this distinction, could complicate effort to define and measure access. Financial market imperfections, such as information asymmetries and transaction cost, were likely to be especially binding on the talented poor and on micro and small enterprises that lacked collateral, credit histories, and connections. Without inclusive financial systems, these individuals and enterprises with promises opportunities were limited to their own savings.

Asian Development Bank (2011) reported that in the 20th century, particularly ADB adopted inclusive economic growth as one of its three critical strategic agendas in Strategy 2020, ADB bank strategy was supporting for inclusive growth in the region through financing, policy advice and knowledge solutions, and technical assistance and capacity building, with particular on building infrastructure, providing basic public services such as water and sanitation and education developing the financial sector and fostering financial inclusion, and enhancing food security.

Asian Development Bank (2011) emphasized that the concept of inclusive growth was economic growth that aimed at high and sustained growth while ensuring that all members of the society benefitted from growth in a high, efficient, and sustained growth to productive job and economic opportunity with equality of life. There were three policy pillars supported by good governance and institutions identified as requirement for a strategy anchored on inclusive growth. The importance of three policy pillar expansion of economics opportunities, and social safety nets supported by good governance and strong institutions, could promote inclusive growth where all members of the society could benefit from and contribute to the growth process.

Sharma et al. (2011) reviewed that increase in GDP alone was not the solution of the deep rooted problem of poverty. Inclusion growth could be a solution for poverty removal. It was concluded from the study that inclusive growth was necessary for sustainable development equitable distribution of wealth and prosperity.

Balbir (2012) found that inclusive growth would act as source of empowerment and allowed people to participate more effectively in the economic and social process. Banks that had global ambitions must meet local aspiration. Financial access would also attract global market players to our country that would result in increasing employment and business opportunities. If we look at the progress that had been achieved, banks were able to scale up and sustain their efforts. India was quite hopeful that the targets set by banks and objective of achieving universal financial inclusion was attainable.

Makarand (2012) revealed that the objective of inclusive growth with stability emphasized in the Eleventh Plan (2007-2012) was not possible without achieving universal Financial Inclusion. The concept of inclusion should be seen as a process of including the excluded agents whose participation was essential in the very design of the development programmes. The bank would really have to gear up in the near future for successful implementation of Financial Inclusion plans. If they were successful in executing the plans, then India could be a role model to the world. Thus, Financial Inclusion was no longer a policy choice today but a policy compulsion.

Soummya et al. (2012) suggested that in order to make financial inclusion successful, a win-win solution set was to be provided to both the parties – the provider and beneficiary. In other words it should be a viable investment alternative to the financial institutions and should also be an attractive on to the borrowers. Financial inclusion was a strategy to achieve the inclusive growth provided it was supported by various factors like real initiatives from and financial institutions, technological development, financial literacy and so on. The role of Central Government and RBI regarding policy making and role of state governments with respect to land settlement rights, providing economic and social infrastructure etc. were very crucial. The time had come to implement policies and schemes adopted by various authorities for rural India to uplift its standards of living and to include it within the periphery of basic financial services. Attempts, therefore, should be made at the grass root level to implement those ideas keeping in mind the panoramic view of inclusive growth prevailing in India.

Studies Based on the Initiatives Taken for Financial Inclusion in India

Chattopadhyan (2011) examined the extent of financial inclusion in West Bengal. The study revealed that there had been an improvement in outreach activity in the banking sector, but the achievement was not significant. An index of financial inclusion (IFI) had been developed in the study using data on three dimensions of financial inclusion-vis banking penetration (BP), availability of the banking services (BS) and usage of the banking system (BU). The study provided a comparable picture between different states on the basis of IFI rankings.

Studies Based on the Problems in Implementation of Financial Inclusion

Collins (2009) studied more than 250 financial diaries of low income individuals in Bangladesh, India, and South Africa. His findings showed that each household used at least four types of informal financial instrument (such as interest free loan and informal savings clubs) in a year, with the average being just under ten. He suggested that low income individuals needed access to financial services, and the existence of barriers that prevent their use of formal sector services. There were many complex factors that prevent rapid progress towards the goal of financial inclusion task force (which monitored access to basic banking services) had differentiated between supply and demand side factors of financial exclusion, in its action plan for 2008-2011. The supply side factors included non-availability of suitable products, physical barriers, and non-eligibility on account of documentation issues. On the demand side, financial literacy and capability were regarded as important sectors by the task force. While financial literacy referred to the basic understanding of financial concept, financial capability referred to the ability and motivation to plan financials, seek out information and advice, and apply them to personal circumstances.

The Financial Action Task Force (FATF), (2011) report summarized the main obstacles to financial inclusion can be summarized as follows:

A. Supply side

- Outreach: low density areas and low income populations were not attractive for the provision of financial services and were not financially sustainable under traditional banking business strategies and corresponding regulatory requirements
- Regulation: framework were not always adapted to local contexts
- Business strategies: mostly with high fixed costs
- Providers: limited number and types of financial service providers
- Services: Non adapted products and services for low income populations and the informal economy

B. Demand side

- Irregular income
- Frequent micro-transactions
- Lack of trust in formal banking institutions
- Literacy level, lack of awareness and/or knowledge/understanding of financial products
- Cultural obstacles (e.g., gender and cultural values)

Manoharan and Krishnavenimuthiah (2010) stated that limited access to affordable financial services such as savings, loan remittance and insurance services to the vast majority of the population in the rural area and unorganized sector was believed to be a constraint to the growth impetus in these sectors. The study was conducted in ten villages of Vadipatti panchayat of Madurai District, Tamilnadu (India). The heads of the family of hundred households were interviewed personally. The behavioral pattern showed that many people were not comfortable using formal financial services. The reasons were difficulty in understanding language, various documents and conditions that come with financial services.

Chhattopadhyay (2012) pointed out that the need for financial inclusion in India perhaps required to be implemented at the earliest and rank next to the priority list of basic infrastructure like good health sanitation and hygiene. Most of our villages were not having bank branches and are still using local post offices for keeping their money in either post office savings schemes or term deposits. Even where the banks and insurance companies had opened their branches, this was used by the rich and influential people depriving other of getting the benefits of such facilities. To such people net transfer, credit cards, plastic money etc. were weird words having no practical meaning to them.

Unnikrishnan et. al (2012) analyzed the importance of financial inclusion in economic empowerment. This study identified the variables in enabling financial inclusion, analyzed the barriers to effective financial inclusion and the prerogative steps to be taken to overcome the barriers and enable inclusive growth. The study concluded by identifying the variables that empowered the masses financially and stating the importance at the bottom of the economic pyramid.

Research Gap

This Research Study was directed towards furthering an understanding of the measures being taken by the Government of India to increase or optimize Financial Inclusion. This study provides the overview of Financial Inclusion Worldwide. As it is reported by Economists, Researchers and Scholars that Inclusive financial systems provide individuals and firms with greater access to resources to meet their financial needs, such as saving for retirement, investing in education, capitalizing on business opportunities, and confronting shocks. But in the Real-world, financial systems are far from inclusive. Indeed, half of the world's adult population lacks a bank account. Many of the world's poor would benefit from financial services but cannot access them due to market failures or inadequate public policies. This Study contributes new data and research that helps fill some of the gaps in knowledge about financial inclusion. It also draws on existing insights and experience to contribute to the policy discussion on this critical development issue. Financial inclusion has moved up the global reform agenda and become a topic of great interest for policy makers, regulators, researchers, market practitioners, and other stakeholders. For the World Bank Group, financial inclusion represents a core topic, given its implications for reducing poverty and boosting shared prosperity. The increased emphasis on financial inclusion reflects a growing realization of its potentially transformative power to accelerate development gains. Financial inclusion is required to uplift the poor and disadvantaged people by providing them the customized financial products and services. This leads to inclusive growth encompassing the deprived and marginalized sections. This study intends to look at the changes occurred in conditions of India by considering the appropriate variables to test. Reserve Bank of India set up the Khan Commission in 2004 to look into financial inclusion and the recommendations of the Commission were incorporated into the mid-term review of the policy (2005-06) and urged banks to review their existing practices to align them with the objective of financial inclusion. However, the progress is far from satisfactory as evidenced by the World

Bank Findex Survey (2012). According to the survey findings, only 35 percent of Indian adults had access to a formal bank account and 8 percent borrowed formally. Only 2 percent of adults used an account to receive money from a family member living in another area and 4 percent used an account to receive payment from the Government. The introduction of a universal and targeted public distribution system (PDS), the provision for employment in rural areas through the National Rural Employment Guarantee Scheme (NREGS), the implementation of the project to bring the population under a unique identification number (AADHAR) and the Direct Benefit Transfer (DBT) Scheme in 2013 are the most recent measures by the government to realize inclusive growth targets.

This research study provides the overview of the global reach of the financial sector—the extent of financial inclusion and the degree to which such groups as the poor, women, and youth are excluded from formal financial systems. This Research Study throws light on the global financial development and growth. It deals with the present scenario of Financial Inclusion Worldwide. It discusses barriers to Financial Inclusion and provides fruitful insight to improve the financial position of the Countries. The present study also attempts to assess the financial inclusion in India and analyses the trends and patterns of economic inequality across Indian states. The basic objective here is to understand the dynamics of growth in the country which is resulting in regional imbalances and propose measures for alleviating the problem.

RESEARCH METHODOLOGY

This Research Study is recognizing the complexity of the questions and the limits of existing knowledge introduces new data and research and draws on available insights and experience to contribute to the policy discussion. The present study is an attempt to find out regional disparity, indebtedness and status of financial inclusion Worldwide with special reference to the initiative taken in India for the betterment of the financial sector. The study is focused on various aspects of Financial Inclusion and it seeks to contribute to the evolving debate on financial inclusion. The present study covers the period from 2000 to 2013. This chapter delineates the statement of problem and research objectives of the present study. It, also, provides insights into the framework and research objectives of the present study. Finally, this chapter outlines the research methodology employed, the way the data for the study has been collected and the statistical tools used for data analysis.

Statement of the Research Problem

Promoting the use of financial services by individuals requires dealing with market failures, such as asymmetric information and moral hazard that prevent the widespread use of financial products. It also involves designing products that fit consumer needs and delivering services at prices that individual can afford. It entails educating and protecting consumers so they avoid making costly mistakes upon entering into financial contracts. Both private sector and government engagement is necessary to expand the financial inclusion of individuals. Technological progress, likely driven by the private sector and facilitated by the public sector, is expected to help increase the financial inclusion of individuals. This research reviews the roles of technology, product design, financial capability, financial education programs, consumer protection and market conduct, and government policies in fostering financial inclusion. Against this backdrop, it was felt that a study on financial inclusion in India would give important clues to understand the nature, causes and determinants of financial inclusion. The objective of the study is primarily to study the causes and determinants of financial inclusion in India.

Research Objectives

Present study is taken up to achieve the following research objectives:

RO1: To study the present status of Financial Inclusion Worldwide.

RO2: To identify the determinants and factors of Financial Inclusion Worldwide.

RO3: To study the issues and challenges of implementation of Financial Inclusion in major part of the World.

RO4: To evaluate the initiatives taken by the various Governments.

RO5: To assess the Financial Inclusion Models implemented by various Governments.

RO6: To identify the technological progress in individuals' Personal Financial Management

RO7: To review the roles of technology and government policies in fostering Financial Inclusion.

RO8: To study the present status of Financial Inclusion in India.

RO9: To identify the determinants of Financial Inclusion in India.

RO10: To assess the regional inequality of Financial Inclusion in India.

RO11: To evaluate the initiatives taken by the Reserve Bank of India in Financial Inclusion.

RO12: To study the issues and challenges of implementation of Financial Inclusion in India.

Execution of Objectives

In this section, Execution of objectives is discussed as follows:

- To accomplish the Research Objective 1-7, the researcher studied the Global Financial Development Report, 2014 published by the World Bank to derive at the particular point of action.
- To attain the Research Objective 8-9, i.e. to study the present status and identify the determinants of financial inclusion in India, the researcher studied the important determinants of financial inclusion which are responsible for inclusive growth of India.
- To attain the Research Objective 10, i.e. to assess the regional inequality of financial inclusion in India, the statistical tool ANOVA (Analysis of Variance) is applied.
- To attain the Research Objective 11, i.e. to evaluate the initiatives taken by the Reserve Bank of India in financial inclusion, Reports of Reserve Bank of India and other relevant studies are discussed.
- To achieve the last Research Objective 12, i.e. to study the issues and challenges of implementation of financial inclusion in India, various studies has been discussed and suggestions have been made to overcome these problems.

Research Plan

This section describes the methodological tools adopted in order to fulfill the research objectives of the present research. Properly conducted research reduces the uncertainty level for the top management in making critical decisions. Hence, it is extremely important to describe the research plan here.

-Research Design

A research design is the specification of methods and procedures for acquiring the needed information. Design to be adopted here is **Descriptive Research**. It basically seeks to extract information about financial inclusion in India as well as World.

-Data Collection

The present research study is based on secondary data. The data is collected from the different websites, as well as different articles, published by the World Bank, the Reserve Bank of India, Government of India, other institutions, research journals and internet. Data from research projects, books and magazines is also discussed. In order to achieve the objectives of the study, secondary data is collected from the Basic Statistical Return of Scheduled Commercial Banks in India (RBI), RBI Monthly Bulletin and Status of Micro Finance in India (NABARD) etc.

-Tools for Data Analysis

The data so collected is analyzed with help of various tools and techniques to fulfill the research objectives. These include ANOVA and Logistic Regression Analysis. The use of these techniques at different places has been made in the light of nature and suitability of data available and requirement of analysis. To conduct the statistical techniques, PASW (Predictive Analytics Software) version 19 for windows and SPSS is used.

CHAPTER PLAN FOR STUDY

The present study is structured around nine chapters. A brief description of each chapter is as follows:

Chapter 1: Introduction

The first chapter highlights the nature and need of the financial inclusion in the process of inclusive growth and explains the importance of financial inclusion in India. This chapter also contains an exhaustive review of the existing literature pertaining to the area of research. The studies have been presented in chronological order so that the latest studies are presented first followed by the subsequent studies. Research gaps have been identified and a case for the present study has been built in the end. Research Methodology proposed to be adopted to fill the research gap has also been defined in this chapter. It defines the statement of problem and research objectives of the present study. It also provides insights into the framework to implement the research objectives of the present study. This chapter also outlines the research methodology employed, the way the data for the study has been collected and the statistical tools used for data analysis.

Chapter 2: World Financial Inclusion

The Second Chapter is focused on the global reach of the financial sector—the extent of financial inclusion and the degree to which such groups as the poor, women, and youth are excluded from formal financial systems. The aim of this chapter is to throw light on the global financial development and growth. It deals with the present scenario of Financial Inclusion Worldwide. It also discusses barriers to Financial Inclusion and provides fruitful insight to improve the financial position of the Countries.

Chapter 3: Financial Inclusion for Individuals' Personal Financial Management

The Third Chapter reviews the roles of technology, product design, financial capability, financial education programs, consumer protection and market conduct, and government policies in fostering financial inclusion.

Chapter 4: Financial Inclusion in India

The Fourth Chapter is focused on the status of financial inclusion in India. The purpose of this chapter is to present an outline of the concept of financial inclusion and its major milestones in India. It also deals with the present scenario of financial inclusion in India.

Chapter 5: Dimension of Financial Inclusion in India

The Fifth Chapter discusses the relationship between financial inclusion and economic development of the country with the help of Index of Financial Inclusion and also explores the factors associated with financial inclusion with the help of Regression Analysis.

Chapter 6:Regional Disparity of Financial Inclusion in India

The Sixth Chapter analyses the trends and patterns of economic inequality across the Indian states. The basic objective here is to understand the dynamics of growth in the country which is resulting in regional imbalances and proposes measures for alleviating the problem. The inter-state inequality in bank branches, credit accounts, saving accounts and credit deposit ratio show a clear picture of regional inequality in India.

Chapter 7: Reserve Bank Initiative for Financial Inclusion in India

The Seventh Chapter critically evaluates the initiatives taken by the Reserve Bank of India for attaining of financial inclusion.

Chapter 8: Issues and Challenges of Financial Inclusion in India

The Eighth Chapter discusses the issues and challenges being faced by banks for achieving a better level of Financial Inclusion in India.

Chapter 9: Recommendations and Conclusion

The conclusion and suggestions emerging from present research are explained in the last Chapter Nine.

Chapter 10: Constraints and Further Area of Research

Limitations of the study and further scope of research area is explained in this chapter.

BIBLIOGRAPHY

CHAPTER TWO

WORLD FINANCIAL INCLUSION

FINANCIAL INCLUSION STATUS: WORLDWIDE

Well-functioning financial systems serve a vital purpose by offering savings, payment, credit, and risk management services to individuals and firms. Inclusive financial systems are those with a high share of individuals and firms that use financial services. Until now little had been known about the global reach of the financial sector—the extent of financial inclusion and the degree to which such groups as the poor, women, and youth are excluded from formal financial systems. Systematic indicators of the use of different financial services had been lacking for most economies. Worldwide, 50 percent of adults report having an individual or joint account at a formal financial institution. But while account penetration is nearly universal in high-income economies, with 89 percent of adults reporting that they have an account at a formal financial institution, it is only 41 percent in developing economies. Globally, more than 2.5 billion adults do not have a formal account, most of them in developing economies. The differences in account ownership by individual characteristics are particularly large in developing economies. While 46 percent of men have a formal account, only 37 percent of women do. Indeed, there is a persistent gender gap of 6–9 percentage points across income groups within developing economies. Among all adults in the developing world, those in the richest quintile (the top 20 percent of the income distribution within an economy) are on average more than twice as likely as those in the poorest to have a formal account.

Unique data on the mechanics of account use across economies show that here too there are sharp differences between high-income and developing economies—in the frequency of deposits and withdrawals, in the way that people access their accounts, and in the payment systems they use. In developing economies 10 percent of adults with a formal account report making no deposits or withdrawals in a typical month; in high-income economies only 2 percent report this. Most account holders in developing economies make deposits and withdrawals primarily through tellers at bank branches; their counterparts in high-income economies rely more heavily on automated teller machines (ATMs). Debit cards, checks, and electronic payments are also far more commonly used in high-income economies.

But there is a bright spot in the expansion of financial services in the developing world: the recent introduction of "mobile money." The greatest success has been in Sub-Saharan Africa, where 16 percent of adults—and 31 percent of those with a formal account—report having used a mobile phone in the past 12 months to pay bills or send or receive money.

The purposes and benefits of account use vary widely. Worldwide, 26 percent of account holders use their account to receive money or payments from the government. This practice is most common in high-income economies and relatively rare in South Asia and East Asia and the Pacific. Compared with counterparts in other parts of the world, adults with a formal account in high-income economies, Europe and Central Asia, and Latin America and the Caribbean are the most likely to report having used their account in the past year to receive wage payments, and those in Sub-Saharan Africa the most likely to report having used their account to receive payments from family members living elsewhere.

Worldwide, 22 percent of adults report having saved at a formal financial institution in the past 12 months, including about half of account holders in high-income economies, Sub-Saharan Africa, and East Asia and the Pacific. In developing economies savings clubs are one common alternative (or complement) to saving at a formal financial institution: in Sub-Saharan Africa 19 percent of adults report having saved in the past year using a savings club or person outside the family. But a large share of adults around the world who report having saved or set aside money in the past 12 months do not report having done so using a formal financial institution, informal savings club, or person outside the family. These adults account for 29 percent of savers worldwide and more than half of savers in 55 economies.

Analysis of Global Findex data shows that account penetration is higher in economies with higher national income as measured by GDP per capita, confirming the findings of previous studies. But national income explains much less of the variation in account penetration for low- and lower-middle-income economies. Indeed, at a given income level and financial depth, use of financial services varies significantly across economies, suggesting a potentially important role for policy.

REMOVING PHYSICAL, BUREAUCRATIC, AND FINANCIAL BARRIERS COULD EXPAND THE USE OF FORMAL ACCOUNTS

Poor people juggle complex financial transactions every day and use sophisticated techniques to manage their finances, whether they use the formal financial system or not. We cannot assume that all those who do not use formal financial services are somehow constrained from participating in the formal financial sector—access and use, are not the same thing. But the recent success of mobile money in Sub-Saharan Africa shows that innovations can bring about dramatic changes in how people engage in financial transactions. To allow a better understanding of the potential barriers to wider financial inclusion, the Global Findex survey includes novel questions on the reasons for not having a formal account. The responses can provide insights into where policy makers might begin to make inroads in expanding the use of formal financial services.

Worldwide, by far the most common reason for not having a formal account—cited by 65 percent of adults without an account—is lack of enough money to use one. This speaks to the fact that having a formal account is not costless in most parts of the world and may be viewed as unnecessary by a person whose income stream is small or irregular. Other common reasons reported for not having an account are that banks or accounts are too expensive (cited by 25 percent of adults without a formal account) and that banks are too far away (cited by 20 percent).

The self-reported barriers vary significantly across regions as well as by individual characteristics. Among adults without a formal account, those in Sub-Saharan Africa and Latin America and the Caribbean are the most likely to cite missing documentation as a reason for not having one. Those in Europe and Central Asia have the least trust in banks. Women tend to report using someone else's account significantly more than do men, highlighting the challenges that women may encounter in account ownership. Adults, who report having saved, but not using a formal account to do so, are significantly more likely to cite distance, cost, and paperwork as barriers to having a formal account.

This systematic evidence on barriers to the use of financial services allows researchers and policy makers to understand reasons for nonuse and to prioritize and design policy interventions accordingly. But because at this point the data are cross-sectional, they cannot be used to determine what impact removing these self-reported barriers would have. Measuring that impact requires rigorous evaluation and is beyond the scope of this report. Moreover, since people often face multiple barriers to the use of formal accounts, and the survey allows multiple responses, addressing individual constraints may not increase the use of accounts if other barriers are binding.

Nevertheless, a cursory look at these self-reported barriers provides interesting information. Distance from a bank is a much greater barrier in rural areas, as expected. Technological and other innovations that help overcome this barrier of physical distance could pay off—potentially increasing the share of adults using a formal account by up to 23 percentage points in Sub-Saharan Africa and 14 percentage points in South Asia. Relaxing documentation requirements could also potentially increase the share of adults with an account by up to 23 percentage points in Sub-Saharan Africa.

Perhaps even more important than barriers of physical access and eligibility are barriers of affordability. These issues seem to be particularly important in Latin America and the Caribbean, where 40 percent of non-account-holders report that formal accounts are too expensive. Worldwide, reducing withdrawal charges and balance fees could make formal accounts more attractive to more than 500 million adults who are without one. Again, these statements are meant to be indicative, not causal, and further analysis is required.

Whether in response to these barriers or for other reasons, many people use informal methods to save money or make payments as an alternative or complement to formal banking. Informal savings clubs and mobile money are two popular examples of financial management tools that can operate outside the formal financial sector.

FORMAL BORROWING AND INSURANCE ARE RELATIVELY RARE IN THE DEVELOPING WORLD

While the share of adults who report having taken out new loans in the past 12 months is surprisingly consistent around the world, the sources and purposes for these loans are extremely diverse. Globally, 9 percent of adults report having originated a new loan from a formal financial institution in the past 12 months—14 percent of adults in high-income economies and 8 percent in developing economies. In addition, about half of adults in high-income economies report having a credit card, which might serve as an alternative to short-term loans. In developing economies only 7 percent report having one. Seven percent of adults around the world have an outstanding mortgage, a share that rises to 24 percent in high-income economies. About 11 percent of adults in developing economies report having an outstanding loan for emergency or health purposes. Less than 20 percent of those in this group report borrowing only from a formal financial institution.

Only 17 percent of adults in developing economies report having personally paid for health insurance, though the share is as low as 2 percent in low-income economies. Of adults working in farming, forestry, or fishing in developing economies, only 6 percent report having purchased crop, rainfall, or livestock insurance in the past year.

BARRIERS TO FINANCIAL INCLUSION (REPORTED IN GLOBAL FINDEX)

Income levels and individual characteristics clearly help explain some of the differences in the use of accounts around the world. What do people say when asked why they do not have an account? The Global Findex survey provides novel data on the barriers to financial inclusion, based on the responses of more than 70,000 adults who do not have a formal account.

Globally, the reason most frequently cited for not having a formal account is the lack of enough money to have and use one (see figure). Thirty percent of adults who are without a formal account cite this as the only reason. The next most commonly cited reason for not having an account is that another family member already has an account. The other reasons reported (in order of importance) are bank accounts being too expensive, excessive distance of banks, lack of the necessary documentation, lack of trust in banks, and religious reasons. Adults in developing economies are significantly more likely to cite distance, cost, documentation, and lack of money compared with adults in developed economies.

The second most frequently cited reason was that another member of the family already has an account, a response that identifies indirect users. Women and adults living in high-income and upper-middle-income economies (where relatives are most likely to have an account) were substantially more likely to choose this reason. A recent study shows that lack of account ownership (and personal asset accumulation) limits women's ability to pursue self-employment opportunities (Hallward-Driemeier and Hasan, 2012). Hence, while such voluntary exclusion may be linked to individual preferences or cultural norms, it may also indicate a lack of awareness of financial products or a lack of financial literacy more generally.

Affordability is a key barrier to account ownership. High costs are cited by a quarter of unbanked respondents, on average, and by 32 percent of unbanked respondents in low-income economies. Fixed transaction costs and annual fees tend to make small transactions unaffordable for large parts of the population. For example, annual fees on a checking account in Sierra Leone are equivalent to 27 percent of GDP per capita. Not surprisingly, 44 percent of adults without accounts in the country cite high cost as a reason for not having a formal account. Analysis finds a significant relationship between cost as a self-reported barrier and objective measures of costs (Demirguc-Kunt and Klapper 2012). Even more importantly, the high costs of opening and maintaining accounts are associated with a lack of competition and underdeveloped physical or institutional infrastructure in a country. This is a key point: it suggests that the high costs associated with a small account do not simply represent the fixed costs of provision, but there is now evidence that some of the costs are associated with underlying distortions (Allen, Demirguc-Kunt, and others 2012).

Twenty percent of unbanked respondents cited distance as a key reason they did not have a formal account. The frequency with which this barrier was cited increases sharply as one moves down the income level of countries, from 10 percent in high-income economies to 28 percent in low-income economies. Among developing economies, there is a significant relationship between distance as a self-reported barrier and objective measures of providers, such as bank branch penetration. To illustrate this point: Tanzania has a large share of non–account-holders who cite distance as a reason they do not have an account—47 percent—and also ranks near the bottom in bank branch penetration, averaging less than 0.5 bank branches per 1,000 square kilometers.

The documentation requirements for opening an account may exclude workers in the rural or informal sector who are less likely to have wage slips or formal proof of residence. There is a significant relationship between subjective and objective measures of documentation requirements as a barrier to account use that holds even after one takes into account GDP per capita (Demirgüç-Kunt and Klapper 2012). Indeed, the Financial Action Task Force, an intergovernmental body aimed at combating money laundering, terrorist financing, and related threats to the integrity of the international financial system, recognized that overly cautious safeguards against money laundering and terrorist financing can have the unintended consequence of excluding legitimate businesses and consumers from financial systems. It has therefore called for such safeguards that also support financial inclusion.

Distrust in formal financial institutions is a nontrivial barrier to wider financial inclusion and one that is difficult to address in the short term. Thirteen percent of adults without a formal account cite lack of trust in banks as a reason for not having an account. This distrust can stem from cultural norms, discrimination against certain segments of the population, past episodes of government expropriation of banks, or economic crises and uncertainty. In Europe and Central Asia, 31 percent of non–account-holders cite lack of trust in banks as a reason for not having an account, a share almost three times the share in other regions, on average.

About 5 percent of unbanked respondents cite religious reasons for not having a formal account. The proportion is higher in some Middle Eastern and South Asian economies, where the development of financial products compatible with religious beliefs (in particular, Islamic finance) could potentially increase account penetration and the use of various financial services.

FINANCIAL SECTOR STRUCTURE, COMPETITION, AND INCLUSION

Which type of financial sector structure works best in reaching out to a broad set of individuals and firms? In terms of financial inclusion and economic development, how do financial systems based on banks compare with those based on financial markets? Studies consistently find that what matters for economic growth is the overall development of the financial system, rather than the relative shares of banks and financial markets. In other words, at similar levels of financial development, more highly bank- or market-oriented economies are not associated with greater economic growth rates, industry growth, or the access of firms to external finance (Beck and Levine 2004; Demirguc-Kunt and Maksimovic 2002; Levine 2002).

While the structure of the financial system does not seem to be associated with growth outcomes, Demirgüç-Kunt and Maksimovic (2002) find that this does affect the types of firms and projects that are financed, which has strong implications for financial inclusion. By looking at firm-level data for 40 countries, they conclude that, in economies with more well developed capital markets, the use by firms of long-term financing is greater. In contrast, firms rely on short-term financing to a much larger extent in countries with more financial structures that are bank-based.

Consistent with these results, Demirgüç- Kunt, Feyen, and Levine (2011) find that financial structures evolve with economic development because capital markets provide financial services that are different than the services provided by banks. Particularly, the significance of market-based financing increases relative to bank-based financing. They show that, as economies develop, the services provided by securities markets become more important for economic activity, while those provided by banks become less important.

Another part of this literature has moved from the market- vs. bank-financing analysis to explore a different angle of financial diversity, more focused on the types of financial institutions (such as niche banks, cooperatives, and MFIs) and their link with access to finance and with economic growth.

In developing economies, the financing needs of a large fraction of households and enterprises are supplied by alternative financial institutions such as cooperatives, credit unions, MFIs, and factoring or leasing companies. While banks are the most prominent institution across regions, their relative importance varies substantially. For instance, for each MFI, there are 46 bank branches in Europe and Central Asia, 32 in Latin America, and only 2 in Sub-Saharan Africa.

Countries also differ in the mix of financial institutions constituting the market because certain types of institutions are more prevalent in particular regions (See figure below). In the Middle East and North Africa, for every 1,000 commercial bank branches, there are 35 cooperatives, 209 state specialized financial institutions, and 44 MFIbranches. However, in Sub-Saharan African countries, there are 480 MFIs for every 1,000 commercial banks, and only 61 cooperative and 37 public bank branches. Countries in Latin America and East Asia and the Pacific are more reliant on cooperatives than are developing countries in other regions. The ratio of cooperatives to bank branches is the highest in upper-income countries, where there are 269 cooperatives per 1,000 commercial bank branches. This pattern is particularly strong in Western European economies, where financial systems rely more on these institutions.

Some argue that a comparative advantage of institutions such as cooperative banks may be that they rely on more flexible lending technologies, making it possible to extract information about more opaque clients, such as micro, small, and medium enterprises or households that do not have available the type of information or documentation that banks traditionally request (Berger, Klapper, and Udell 2001; Stein 2002). Others argue that banks can extend financing to more opaque clients by applying different transactional technologies that facilitate arm's-length lending and that, through more competition, improved financial infrastructure, and appropriate incentives, banks can be encouraged to reach out for new clients (Berger and Udell 2006; de la Torre, Gozzi, and Schmukler 2007).

A study by Beck, Demirguc-Kunt, and Singer (forthcoming) explores the role of different kinds of financial institutions, as well as their average size, in easing the access of firms to financial services and finds heterogeneous impacts across countries and firm sizes. More specifically, in low-income countries, a higher share of low-end financial institutions (such as cooperatives, credit unions, and MFIs) and specialized lenders (such as factoring and leasing companies) is associated with better access to finance. The evidence the authors present indicates that the average size of financial institutions matters for inclusion. In contrast to earlier studies suggesting that smaller financial institutions are better able to serve the credit needs of small, opaque borrowers (for example, Berger and Udell 1995; Keeton 1995), the authors reject that smaller institutions are better at easing the access of firms to finance. On the contrary, in countries with low levels of GDP per capita, larger banks and low-end institutions seem to improve access to financial services, and larger banks and specialized lenders seem to facilitate access to loans and overdraft use by smaller enterprises.

These results are in line with the findings of more recent studies. For instance, Berger, Klapper, and Udell (2001) find that larger banks may be as well equipped as smaller ones to serve small clients because they use a different lending technology. De la Torre, Gozzi, and Schmukler (2007) likewise find that, contrary to the belief that large banks are less capable of reaching out to opaque small and medium enterprises, most banks find such enterprises profitable for several reasons. One such reason is the increased use of different transactional technologies that benefit from the economies of scale of larger institutions (for example, the use of credit scoring models requires a large pool of clients, thereby benefiting from larger bank size).

Relationship lending is one of several other ways in which banks extend financing to more opaque clients (Berger and Udell 2006). Two examples of large banks that have adopted innovative lending technologies and business models are Banco Azteca in Mexico and BancoSol in Bolivia. BancoSol is arguably the first commercial bank to specialize in microfinance. Its lending technology relies on a solidarity group lending strategy, whereby members organize small joint liability credit groups, and the bank lends simultaneously to all group members (Gonzalez-Vega and others 1997). Banco Azteca, on the other hand, targets clients employed in the informal sector by using their durable goods as collateral for loans. Ruiz (2013) shows that, in municipalities in which this bank has opened a branch, households with members working in the informal sector are more likely to borrow from banks, are less likely to rely on more expensive credit suppliers, and are thus better able to smooth their consumption and accumulate more valuable durable goods.

Beyond financial structure, evidence points to competition in the financial sector as a key factor in enhancing financial inclusion. Examining firm-level data for 53 countries from 2002 to 2010, Love and Martínez Pería (2012) find that bank competition substantially increases the access of firms to finance. An advantage of their study relative to others is that their data allow them to isolate within-country variations in competition and access to finance more effectively. In a more micro level analysis, Lewis, Morais, and Ruiz (2013) examine competition among Mexican banks. Their results show that large banks are more likely to engage in less competitive practices and confirm that, as expected, competition leads to less collusive practices. Importantly, less competition disproportionally affects access to finance among smaller firms.

To summarize, recent studies indicate more financially diverse markets are associated with improved access to finance. Policy recommendations to support a more financially diverse landscape encompass (1) improving competition within the financial system, but also allowing a variety of financial institutions to operate (from specialized lenders and low-end institutions to banks with lending technologies or business models that reach out to new clients in responsible ways); (2) strengthening financial and lending infrastructure, including commercial laws, bankruptcy laws, and contract enforcement; and (3) creating the conditions for capital market development to improve access to longer-term finance.

PUBLIC AND PRIVATE SECTOR BREAKTHROUGHS IN FINANCIAL INCLUSION

There is clear potential for private sector and public sector led breakthroughs in expanding financial inclusion. For example, the Global Findex data show that, in Kenya, 68 percent of adults report they had used a mobile phone in the past 12 months to pay bills or send or receive money. The spread of mobile money products, the proliferation of bank agents, and the growing movement toward dispensing government payments via formal accounts all offer potential to alter substantially the ways in which adults manage their day-to-day finances.

The public sector can bring about change in how adults around the globe interact with the formal financial sector. Increasingly, governments are using formal accounts to disburse transfer payments. In Brazil, the government allows recipients of conditional cash transfers (as part of its Bolsa Familia Program) to receive payments via no-frills bank accounts, though many more choose to receive payments via a virtual account that does not allow deposits or indefinite storage. Still, 20 percent of adults in Brazil report receiving government transfers via a bank account, among the highest rates in the developing world. In India, the government recently began depositing government pension and scholarship payments directly into the bank accounts of almost 250,000 people in 20 districts; officials plan to expand the program with the aim of preventing corruption as well as increasing financial access. These types of reforms have the potential to extend the reach of the formal financial sector to the poorest individuals.

The challenge for public policy is to ensure that enhancements in access are achieved through the removal of market and regulatory distortions rather than through price regulation or other anticompetitive policies that may exacerbate distortions and threaten financial stability. Policies can enhance financial inclusion by addressing imperfections in the supply of financial services (for example, through modern payment and credit information systems, the use of new lending technologies, support for competition in the provision of financial services) and in the demand for financial services (for instance, through financial literacy initiatives that raise awareness and lead to the more responsible use of finance). Policies to support financial inclusion also include initiatives to remove nonmarket barriers that prevent equitable access to financial services (for example, through consumer protection and antidiscrimination laws). More generally, the challenge for policy is to guarantee that financial service providers are delivering their services as widely and inclusively as possible and that the use of such services is not hampered by inappropriate regulatory policies or nonmarket barriers that limit the use of financial services.

There are many important links between the public sector and financial inclusion. Weak public sector institutions are detrimental to financial inclusion; so, improvements in public sector governance can have a positive impact on the use of and the access to financial services in an equitable way. There are also key effects in the other direction: if electronic payments are widely available, this can boost the efficiency of public sector programs.

CHAPTER THREE

FINANCIAL INCLUSION FOR INDIVIDUALS' PERSONAL FINANCIAL MANAGEMENT

Promoting the use of financial services by individuals requires dealing with market failures, such as asymmetric information and moral hazard that prevent the widespread use of financial products. It also involves designing products that fit consumer needs and delivering services at prices that individuals can afford. It entails educating and protecting consumers so they avoid making costly mistakes upon entering into financial contracts. Both private sector and government engagement is necessary to expand the financial inclusion of individuals. Technological progress, likely driven by the private sector and facilitated by the public sector, is expected to help increase the financial inclusion of individuals. This chapter reviews the roles of technology, product design, financial capability, financial education programs, consumer protection and market conduct, and government policies in fostering financial inclusion.

THE ROLE OF TECHNOLOGY

The last two decades have seen a proliferation of new technologies with significant potential to improve financial access. As illustrated in previous chapter, transaction costs and geographical barriers are major impediments to the provision of financial services. Innovative technologies-including mobile banking, electronic credit information systems, and biometric individual identification-can reduce such transaction costs and can thus help overcome some of the traditional barriers to financial access.

Major innovations in retail payment systems date back to the rise of card-based payment services. Credit cards were introduced in the 1950s, and their use grew rapidly over the next three decades based on infrastructure developed and managed mainly by the card associations Visa and MasterCard. During the late 1980s and the 1990s, because of growing sophistication in information processing and telecommunications technologies which among other features, allowed online transaction authorization by issuers, credit cards became a widely accepted form of payment in many countries. In the 1980s, debit cards started to evolve as a key electronic payment instrument. Today, in some countries where credit card adoption has been slow because of the limited infrastructure for credit information and other issues, such as cultural preferences, debit cards have become the most popular electronic instrument for retail payments. The growth in debit cards has been dramatic over the last 25–30 years. At first, debit cards were enablers for moving customers from bank teller counters to the newly deployed automatic teller machine (ATM) systems. Over time, instead of using the card to withdraw cash from an ATM to pay merchants, bank customers could simply present the card to the merchants and have their bank account debited directly. Given this tremendous potential, debit card products evolved globally and became based on the infrastructure that was already in place for processing credit card transactions at the point of sale.

The market for prepaid cards, or stored value cards, has also become one of the most rapidly growing segments in the retail payment industry. In the 1990s, when prepaid cards first became available, they were mostly issued by non-financial businesses and used in limited deployment environments, such as mass transportation systems. In recent years, prepaid cards have grown substantially as financial institutions and nonbank organizations target the unbanked and migrant remittance segments of populations. Some prepaid cards already rely on the existing infrastructure for traditional credit and debit cards. Technological innovations in the way information is stored (such as magnetic stripe or computer chip), the physical form of the payment mechanism, and biometric account access and authentication are converging to create efficiencies, reduce transaction times at the point of sale, and lower transaction costs.

Although innovations in card-based retail payments have expanded access to finance and the method remains a dominant mode of transactions in many countries, there are limitations. From a consumer protection perspective, card-based payment systems can be problematic because of hidden, nontransparent fees. From a technology perspective, a potential concern is that the huge investments that banks and payment system providers have made into card-based payment infrastructure may inhibit interoperability and create market segmentation, which may have negative implications for competition and product innovation.

More recently, much attention has been focused on the role of mobile banking applications in financial inclusion. The reason is that mobile phones have been adopted by consumers at a rapid rate, becoming almost ubiquitous. They are now well within the reach of many poor individuals around the world. In many low- and middle-income countries, the share of the population that has access to a mobile phone is considerably larger than the share of the population that has a formal bank account. For example, in 2011, there were 127 mobile phone subscriptions for every 100 inhabitants in South Africa, while only 54 percent of the population had a bank account. There were 123 mobile phone subscriptions per 100 inhabitants in Brazil, while only 56 percent had a bank account. And, in India, 72 of every 100 inhabitants had a mobile phone, while only 35 percent had a bank account. These numbers illustrate the vast potential of mobile telephony to enhance financial inclusion.

Mobile banking has been perhaps the most visible example of the use of new technologies to advance financial inclusion, but new technologies have also had an impact in other areas. For instance, modern information technologies have allowed banks to serve previously unbanked locations through banking correspondents. Improved technologies for credit reporting and borrower identification have dramatically reduced the cost of financial intermediation and allowed banks to provide financial services to clients who would have been excluded from the use of formal financial services in the absence of these technologies. As computing power has grown, banks are also able to leverage data on historical client behavior to better assess credit risk and deliver credit to previously underserved individuals.

While new technologies are, in principle, available globally, their adoption and use for financial inclusion have been uneven across countries, and there has also been great variation in whether such technologies have been pioneered by the traditional financial sector or other players. India's financial inclusion strategy, for example, relies on providing basic financial services through traditional bank branches and technologically based correspondent banking, both led by the country's large public sector banks. At the other end of the spectrum, Kenya's popular mobile payment service, M-PESA, is operated by a private telecommunications provider and has reached nationwide appeal independently of the traditional banking sector.

This section discusses the role of technology in financial inclusion. It reviews the growth of mobile banking and payment systems and discusses technology-based business models and the role of improved borrower identification and credit reporting technologies in financial inclusion. The section highlights that technology-based strategies for financial inclusion have varied substantially across countries and examines the features of national market environments that determine which technologies are best suited to enhance financial inclusion, as well as issues related to market structure and regulation that might make the success of some technology-based solutions difficult to replicate elsewhere.

Mobile banking and payments

Mobile banking and payment technologies are among the most significant financial sector innovations of the last decades. The wide geographical reach and the rapid growth of mobile phone technology has dramatically reduced communication costs from prohibitive levels to prices that are well within the reach of many low- and middle-income individuals across the developing world. In the early stages of this technological revolution, users started transferring air time credits as a mode of payment within the network. This soon gave rise to the first mobile payment systems that were formalized by telecommunications providers (such as Safaricom in Kenya) or by banks that began allowing customers to receive, transfer, and deposit money over the mobile phone network.

There is still considerable scope for expansion in mobile technology to translate into greater access to financial services. For example, Alonso and others (2013), using data on Mexico, estimate the potential demand gap for mobile banking—the difference between the possession of mobile phones and the access to current bank accounts—at about 40 percent.

To put matters in perspective, although mobile money has changed the economics of banking across the globe, the aggregate volumes of mobile banking transactions are still small compared with the value transacted through traditional payment instruments. Returning to the example of Kenya, one of the countries where the adoption of mobile payments has been most successful, the value of transactions among banks is nearly 700 times larger than the value of all transactions among M-PESA mobile accounts (Jack and Suri, 2011).

One area where mobile technologies can be an important driver of change is remittance flows. While mobile payments are becoming a popular channel for sending domestic remittances, technological and regulatory barriers still constrain their widespread use for international remittances. Mobile banking and payment technologies could serve as a key stepping-stone into the use of formal financial services, but a major challenge is to design secure mobile applications in a way that makes them easy to access and use in everyday transactions. Because mobile banking and payment applications have network externalities, they become more cost effective to operate and use as more participants join the system. In practice, this means that the success of mobile banking and payment systems depends crucially on the number of potential users a participant can transact with. Because mobile money applications in developing countries are set up in the context of what are still largely cash economies, other crucial factors determining their adoption are the number of cash-in points and the ease with which cash can be transferred into and out of the mobile system.

What are some of the requirements that would need to be in place for a country to replicate Kenya's extraordinarily successful experience in the adoption of mobile payments? The economics of mobile banking rely on network externalities and economies of scale. In the case of Kenya, the rapid adoption of mobile banking was driven by Safaricom, the largest mobile network operator in the country, which provided an extensive network that ensured banking was viable for the provider as well as for potential clients. In settings where the market for mobile banking is more fragmented, the adoption of these technologies has often been much slower because providers have insufficient incentives to invest in the extensive infrastructure required to make mobile banking economically viable.

This illustrates that regulators walk a fine line between providing incentives for the development of mobile payment platforms and requiring these platforms to be open. From a consumer perspective, it is clearly desirable to require different electronic banking and payment platforms to be interoperable so that users can interact across mobile banking applications without technological barriers or extra charges. However, if operators are required to interconnect at an early stage of development, this may weaken the incentives to invest in infrastructure and services that can be leveraged throughout the system. Striking the right balance between these competing policy goals remains a key challenge in the regulation of new payment technologies.

Aside from issues of market structure and regulation, there are a variety of government policies that can support the adoption of mobile banking. One policy that has been showing some promise in encouraging the adoption of mobile banking technologies is the use of government-to-person (G2P) payments. G2P payments provide an attractive opportunity to draw previously unbanked beneficiaries into formal financial services by channeling a consistent flow of money into financial accounts. Several governments have begun to experiment with the use of mobile payment technologies on a small scale, for example, as a way to channel welfare payments to low-income individuals. These are only relatively limited programs in terms of size and aggregate effect so far; most governments use card-based or direct deposit technologies for G2P payments. However, two instances of large government transfer programs that have gone fully mobile are Colombia's Familias en Accion Program and Pakistan's Benazir Income Support Program.

The digitalization of government payments in Pakistan is an example of how G2P payments over mobile networks can be used as an effective tool for supporting financial inclusion. There are currently 1.8 million mobile banking accounts in Pakistan and more than 31,000 agents (covering 90 percent of Pakistan's districts) who process more than 10 million payments per month. Several mobile banking providers currently operate in Pakistan, and nearly all of them are involved in the digitized disbursement of G2P payments (Rotman, Kumar, and Parada 2013). The case of Pakistan is also a good example of how governments can work with private sector partners to leverage the benefits of mobile banking technologies: Pakistan's government agencies are keen to channel G2P payments through mobile banking to reduce administrative costs and increase transparency, while mobile banking providers view G2P payments as a useful way to grow their client base among low- and middle-income individuals. As a result, the share of G2P payments made through Pakistan's mobile network has steadily risen, and it is expected that, within five years, up to 75 percent of all G2P payments in Pakistan could be digitized.

The effect of mobile banking on savings has been a matter of some dispute. Because many mobile banking platforms were originally designed as pure payment systems, one concern is that mobile banking facilitates payments and consumption but does not generate incentives to save and to engage in other welfare-enhancing financial behaviors. There is some evidence that mobile banking services are used much more as a mode of transaction than as a store of value. For example, in a study of mobile banking in Kenya, Mbiti and Weil (2011) suggest that access to M-PESA has only a limited effect on the ability of individuals to save. In a related study, Demombynes and Thegeya (2012) show that enrollment in Kenya's M-PESA system increases the likelihood of saving by up to 20 percentage points. People who have only M-PESA save, on average, K Sh 1,305 per month (about $13), compared with K Sh 2,282 per month among people who save only with other accounts and K Sh 2,959 among people who save with M-PESA and other accounts.

Taking into consideration the fact that people who save using non–M-PESA accounts tend to be wealthier individuals who save more, one may conclude that mobile banking—in addition to reaching unprecedented numbers of low-income individuals with basic payment services—may encourage savings. Reliable evidence on this point is, however, scarce. One reason for this is that many electronic retail payment systems still focus heavily on facilitating transactions, but do not offer sufficiently attractive savings products. In some cases, this is because regulators do not permit mobile banking providers to act as deposit-taking institutions. There is, nonetheless, wide variation in regulatory regimes, and some providers, such as M-Shwari in Kenya, have partnered with banks and started offering credit products.

Innovative delivery channels

In addition to enhancing financial inclusion directly, new mobile banking and payment technologies have also given rise to technology-based business models that can broaden access to basic financial services. Banking correspondents that use a combination of card- and mobile-based technologies are an example of how banks use new technologies to provide financial services to previously unbanked customers and locations.

A banking correspondent is a representative of a bank who operates transactions on behalf of one or more banks outside the bank's branch network. The term "banking correspondent" is often used broadly and may include post offices, supermarkets, grocery stores, gasoline stations, and lottery outlets that offer basic financial services. Banking correspondents can be fixed retail locations that offer banking services to clients on a commission basis in previously unbanked locations or mobile banking agents that visit remote locations regularly to offer basic financial services. It is worth distinguishing between banking correspondents, who offer a broader range of financial services on behalf of a bank, and mobile agents, who act on behalf of a mobile phone or payment operator and typically provide only elementary transaction services. Both types of correspondent models have grown rapidly through the advent of new mobile banking and payment technologies. They rely on mobile banking and point-of-sale technologies to reduce transaction costs and expand access to financial services beyond locations covered by a bank's existing network of branches.

The innovative aspect of mobile technology–based correspondent banking is the combination of mobile technologies and new delivery channels, for example, by using retail outlets as banking correspondents. This enables banks to offer more convenient points of access to existing customers, decongest their branches, collect payments, and gain a larger geographical presence without having to invest in brick and mortar branches. Most of the underlying technologies are similar to those that enable basic mobile banking. However, correspondent banking can also reach people without mobile phones. Moreover, it typically provides a broader suite of financial services—including insurance and savings products—than mobile banking. More recently, some of the more mature mobile payment platforms have linked up with banking partners to offer a broader range of products to customers, often through the retail channel of an established banking correspondent network.

Evidence shows that correspondent banking has had a substantial impact on financial inclusion. For example, Allen, Demirgüç-Kunt, and others (2012) find that, among adults in the bottom income quintile, the likelihood of using a formal financial account increases by up to 5 percentage points through the introduction of correspondent banking.

In many countries, including Brazil, India, Kenya, and Mexico, correspondent banking has been instrumental in enhancing the access to basic financial services. For instance, technology-based business models played a key part in India's policies to enhance financial inclusion. In 2006, India adopted a bank led, technology-driven banking correspondent model. The Reserve Bank of India called on banks to provide basic financial services in all unbanked villages in two phases: first, to all villages with a population of at least 2,000 and, second, to all villages with a population of less than 2,000. Banks have used a combination of new branches, fixed location business correspondent outlets, and mobile technology–based banking correspondents to meet this target. As of March 2012, 96,828 new customer service points had been set up under the program. According to Findex data, only about 35 percent of India's adult population had a bank account in 2011.

Brazil leads the way globally in terms of the coverage and number of correspondents. Brazil's strong payment system infrastructure has set the technological foundation for the successful and rapid deployment of correspondent banking. Brazil has 1,471 point of sale terminals per 100,000 adults, more than three times the number in Chile (450 per 100,000), and also leads the region in ATMs, at 121 per 100,000, a coverage rate similar to the rates in Germany and other European countries. The large government transfer programs handled through public banks have also created an immediate use for the correspondent networks. Today, these are largely grouped under the Bolsa Familia conditional cash transfer program, which serves nearly 14 million families (the largest program of its kind in the developing world). Central bank regulations likewise encourage financial institutions to reach out to more distant consumers and to communities where they had not previously been active. The Brazilian example illustrates not only the enormous successes, but also some of the challenges that this innovative channel faces. For example, despite progress, correspondents in poorer and more remote areas tend to be limited to providing basic access to payments, and services such as savings, credit, and insurance are not readily available for many low-income consumers.

GOVERNMENT POLICIES FOR FINANCIAL INCLUSION

A key role for the government in terms of financial inclusion is to deal with obstacles in the supply or demand of financial services that can lead to inefficient outcomes. For example, a bank investing in a technology or business model that can reach underserved customers has to bear the risks and the initial costs if the experiment fails, but can quickly lose market share if others follow its lead. Problems of this sort can promote underinvestment in innovations that can mitigate asymmetric information and high transaction costs. At the same time, the departures of consumers from rational behavior may also generate inefficient outcomes and justify government action.

The following subsections focus on three roles that the government can play in financial inclusion to mitigate the problems associated with asymmetric information, high transaction costs, and consumer irrationality: (1) develop the legal and regulatory framework, (2) support the information environment, and (3) subsidize access or undertake other direct policies to expand financial inclusion.

Developing the Legal and Regulatory Framework

Legal institutions underpin the development of the financial sector (Djankov, McLiesh, and Shleifer 2007; La Porta and others 1997, 1998; Levine 1998, 1999). In particular, the protection of private property and the enforcement of shareholder and creditor rights are cornerstones of developed financial sectors (for example, see Levine 1998, 1999). In environments with weak legal institutions, contract writing and enforcement are problematic. As a result, financial institutions tend to resort to more costly business models (such as relationship lending or group monitoring) that might limit both the supply and the demand for their services.

The government has a key part in enhancing financial inclusion by introducing laws that protect property and creditor rights and by making sure that these laws are adequately enforced. A number of studies find that both the quality of the laws and the efficiency of enforcement of creditor rights affect the availability and cost of credit to households. Meador (1982) finds that interest rates in the U.S. mortgage market are higher in those states in which the cost and duration of judicial interventions to repossess collateral are greater. Focusing on Europe, Freixas (1991) shows that the cost and the duration of the judicial process required to repossess collateralized assets are inversely related to consumer and home lending. Combining data on Italian households and the performance of Italian judicial districts, Fabbri and Padula (2004) find that an increment in the backlog of pending trials has a statistically and economically significant positive effect on the probability of loan rejections among households. Japelli, Pagano, and Bianco (2005) find similar evidence using aggregate credit data across 95 Italian provinces. Using data on mortgage debt outstanding in 62 countries during 2001–05, Warnock and Warnock (2008) find that countries with stronger protections for legal rights have deeper housing finance systems.

The efficiency of the legal system also matters because this can affect the sectoral composition of lending. For instance, Costa and de Mello (2006) find that, in Brazil, banks provided payroll loans—the repayment of which was deducted from the employee's payroll check—at lower rates than regular consumer loans, which were subject to the inefficient procedures of the Brazilian legal system. Using databank-level survey data for over 20 transition economies, Haselmann and Wachtel (2010) find that, if bankers have positive perceptions of the legal environment, they tend to lend more to opaque borrowers such as households and small and medium enterprises.

The strength and enforcement of creditor rights can have implications for household debt repayment behavior. Using data from the European Community Household Panel during 1994–2001, Duygan-Bump and Grant (2009) find that, if faced with adverse shocks, households in countries with poor protection of creditor rights are more likely to delay their loan repayments. Hence, poorly designed and enforced creditor rights discourage lending and encourage households to default.

A key component of a modern collateral framework is the existence of collateral registries. The extensive research on the use of property rights, land titles, and access to finance suggests that property ownership is important in the attitudes, beliefs, and behaviors that can have a considerable impact on a variety of social, income, and even environmental factors (Di Tella, Galiani, and Schargrodsky 2007; Goldstein and Udry 2008; Jacoby, Li, and Rozelle 2002). However, the traditional view of the importance of property rights in access to finance arising because property provides solid collateral is being challenged by new findings. For example, Deininger and Goyal (2012) evaluate the impact of modernizing land title registries in Andhra Pradesh, India, and find significant, but modest rises in access to credit only in urban areas. Galiani and Schargrodsky (2010) study the impact of the acquisition of clear land titles on access to finance and on other measures of well-being in a poor suburban area of Buenos Aires. They find that household welfare improves, but not through the credit channel; rather, long-term investments in housing and human capital formation made without access to formal credit account for the changes. Galiani and Schargrodsky (2011a) discuss the difficulty that low-income homeowners face in maintaining formal land titles over time because of the relatively high cost of the administrative procedures. Galiani and Schargrodsky (2011b) fi nd evidence of links between long-term investments and stronger property rights in rural areas, but none of the links are attributable to the use of land for collateral in formal credit markets. These studies point to the importance of strong property rights, but call into question policies focused narrowly on providing land titles.

Developing the information environment

Information asymmetries between people who demand and people who supply financial services can lead to adverse selection and moral hazard. For example, in credit markets, adverse selection arises when information about the borrower's characteristics is unknown to the lender. Moral hazard refers to a situation whereby the lender's inability to observe a borrower's actions that affect repayment might lead to opportunistic behavior on the part of the borrower. In both cases, asymmetric information leads to rationing (a situation where the supply falls short of the demand).

The government can enhance financial inclusion by facilitating the access of banks to borrower information either by passing laws and regulations that enable banks to share information or by directly setting up public credit registries. These are databases established and managed by central banks or financial supervisors that capture information on both individual and firm borrowers and their credit. Private credit bureaus refer, meanwhile, to information-sharing arrangements spontaneously created and maintained by private financial institutions.

Subsidies and Debt Relief Programs

As in other areas of development, the use of public funds is easy to justify in the interest of improving access and thereby promoting pro poor growth. Such subsidies should be evaluated against the many alternative uses of the donor funds or scarce public funds, not least of which are alternative subsidies to meet the education, health, and other priority needs among the poor. In practice, such a cost benefit calculation is rarely made. Indeed, the scale of subsidies is often unmeasured.

Furthermore, as with financial sector taxation, subsidies can be more liable to deadweight costs in finance than in many other sectors (Honohan 2003). It is often especially difficult to ensure that finance-related subsidies reach the target group or have the hoped for effect.

An even more serious problem is the possible chilling effect of subsidies on the commercial provision of competing and potentially better services for the poor. Subsidizing finance is likely to undermine the motivation and incentive for market-driven financial firms to innovate and deliver. It is this danger-that subsidies will inhibit the viability of sustainable financial innovation—that can be the decisive argument against some forms of subsidy.

Note that it is not subsidization of the poor that should be questioned: the poor need help and subsidies in many dimensions. Subsidies to cover fixed costs (for example, in payment systems, especially if these generates network externalities) may be less subject to this chilling effect than subsidies that operate to cover marginal costs. Each case must be assessed on the merits.

Other direct interventions to address Financial Inclusion

Several other direct interventions for financial inclusion have attracted attention in recent years. These include government-to-person (G2P) payments, the use of state-owned banks, the use of government postal services for financial inclusion, and explicit financial inclusion strategies.

In the payments and savings arena, governments can potentially play a direct role in enhancing financial inclusion by using G2P payments to raise the demand for bank accounts. These payments, which could include social transfers and wage and pension payments, can facilitate access through existing government infrastructure, such as post office networks. If well designed, these payments have the potential to become a vehicle for extending financial inclusion, and some observers have noted that providing poor G2P recipients with financial services could strengthen the development impact of G2P payments (Bold, Porteous, and Rotman 2012; Pickens, Porteous, and Rotman 2009). Allen, Demirgüç-Kunt, and others (2012) examine the effects of G2P payments as part of a broader examination of the factors driving financial inclusion. Specifically, they include in their models of account penetration a dummy variable for whether the government reported it had encouraged or mandated the payment of government transfers or social payments through bank accounts. They find that the existence of accounts to receive G2P payments lowers the likelihood that the individuals with the accounts will cite lack of funds as a barrier. This suggests that government policies to enhance inclusion can increase the likelihood that individuals perceive that financial services are within their reach. There is growing evidence that postal networks can play a powerful role in financial inclusion. According to some observers, postal networks around the world have gone or are going through a transformation from mail-centered bureaucracies to diversified commercial enterprises with a social mission to serve the whole population and reduce financial exclusion (Berthaud and Davico 2013; El-Zoghbi and Martinez 2012). The arrival of the Global Findex data provides some new cross-country empirical evidence on the subject, suggesting where postal financial inclusion may be relevant and applicable. The data show that postal financial inclusion reaches the poorer, older, less well educated and unemployed people at the bottom of the pyramid.

Financial Inclusion Strategies

A growing number of countries have adopted formal national financial inclusion strategies. These are public documents, developed through a consultative process that typically involves a variety of public sector bodies (the ministry of finance or economy, the central bank, consumer protection agencies, the ministry of justice, social protection agencies, and so on) as well as private sector firms (commercial banks, insurance firms, nonbank financial institutions, telecommunications firms), and civil society partners (such as microfinance organizations and nongovernmental organizations in financial education). In many countries, the financial inclusion strategy is led by the central bank. In Kenya, for example, the central bank was aided by Financial Sector Deepening Trusts, supported by the United Kingdom's Department for International Development, and surveys and research conducted by Finmark Trust. In Colombia, a government-created independent trust fund has led efforts on financial access.

The main stated objective of these strategies is to increase the access to finance. A typical strategy would highlight a headline target. For example, Nigeria's strategy, published in October 2012, aims to reduce financial exclusion in the country from 46 percent to 20 percent by 2020. Beyond the headline target, the strategy defines financial inclusion, identifies key stakeholders, outlines their roles and responsibilities, reports on the status of financial inclusion in Nigeria relative to international benchmarks, discusses barriers to financial inclusion, introduces a range of targets, presents a range of strategies for achieving financial inclusion targets, discusses the implications for regulation and policy in Nigeria, introduces regular monitoring and evaluation, and puts in place an organizational framework for the institutionalization of the strategy. Notably, the strategy sets rather specific targets for payments, savings, credit, insurance, pensions, branches of deposit banks and microfinance banks, and so on. The key initiatives in the strategy include a tiered approach to spreading awareness of customer rules, agent banking, mobile payments, cashless policies, the financial literacy framework, consumer protection, and the implementation of credit enhancement schemes and programs.

The Alliance for Financial Inclusion, a global network of financial policy makers from developing and emerging countries, has begun a Policy Champion Program to promote dissemination of good practices. In 2012, alliance member states issued the Maya Declaration, the first global and measurable set of commitments by developing and emerging country governments to unlock the economic and social potential of the 2.5 billion unbanked people worldwide through greater financial inclusion. More than 40 countries have signed the declaration.

An important perceived benefit of these strategy documents is better coordination of multiple stakeholders and initiatives. Indeed, most country authorities report that the consultative process involved in preparing the strategies leads to improved dialogue and better coordination among multiple stakeholders and initiatives, greater knowledge of the sector, and clearer commitments to good practices.

Evidence on the effectiveness of the national financial inclusion strategies is still only emerging. Dufl os and Glisovic-Mézières (2008) discuss national microfinance strategies in some 30 countries, mostly in Africa, pointing out that usually the strategies have been initiated at the request of donors. They find little evidence that the strategies have influenced access to finance in the countries where they have been adopted. They identify some challenges, such as weak diagnostics, inadequate government leadership, and unrealistic action plans. The paper offers suggestions to donors on the development of the strategies. These include investing in comprehensive sector diagnostics (so that the strategy is based on solid data), analyzing the political climate, ensuring local ownership, evaluating results, and being open to changing course. A recently published framework document for financial inclusion strategies describes how selected countries have approached this task and provides general guidance for nations that may be contemplating such strategy exercises (World Bank 2012i).

While it is still too early to perform a rigorous examination of these strategies, there are some initial signs that improvements can be achieved through shared public and private sector commitments to financial inclusion. For example, the South Africa Financial Sector Charter helped raise the percentage of banked adults from 46 to 64 percent in four years, and six million basic bank accounts (called Mzansi accounts) were opened. In the United Kingdom, a Financial Inclusion Taskforce contributed to halving the number of unbanked adults through e-money regulation, G2P payments linked to bank accounts, and access to financial services through post offices. The government of Brazil implemented regulatory reforms that enabled the financial sector to respond with innovative products and enhance access, leading to a dramatic expansion in financial service access points. As a result, every municipality in the country, including in remote rural areas, is now covered.

KEY MESSAGES TO POLICY-MAKERS

- **Promoting the use of financial services by individuals requires that market distortions**-such as information asymmetries or the abuse of market power-preventing the widespread use of financial products be addressed, ways be found to deliver services at lower costs for suppliers and consumers, and consumers be educated and protected so they use products that meet their needs and avoid costly mistakes. Governments can confront market failures and enhance inclusion by developing an appropriate legal and regulatory framework, supporting the information environment, promoting competition, and facilitating the adoption of business models by providers to enhance financial inclusion.

- **Technological advances hold promise in the expansion of financial inclusion.** Transaction costs become an obstacle for financial inclusion if providers cannot profitably serve low income consumers. Innovations in technology, such as mobile banking, mobile payments, and the biometric identification of individuals, help reduce transaction costs. Which technology is appropriate for financial inclusion depends on the development of the traditional banking sector; market size, structure, and density; and the level of development of supporting infrastructure.
- **Product designs that deal with market failures, meet consumer needs, and overcome behavioral problems can foster the widespread use of financial services.** Certain business models and delivery channels can also enhance inclusion by reducing the cost of using financial services. The regulatory stance of governments can influence the product designs and business models of financial institutions. Hence, governments should strike a delicate balance between financial stability concerns and supporting innovations in product design and business models that allow for greater financial inclusion.
- **How best to strengthen financial capability, that is, financial knowledge, skills, attitudes, and behaviors, remains a focus of research and discussion, but some lessons are emerging:** the importance of using teachable moments to deliver financial knowledge, the value of social networks (such as between parents and children or between remittance senders and receivers), the relevance of psychological traits such as impulse control, and the possible benefits of new delivery channels such as entertainment education and text messaging.
- **Evidence points to the role of government in setting standards for disclosure and transparency, regulating aspects of business conduct, and overseeing effective recourse mechanisms to protect consumers.** To avoid conflicts of interest, prudential regulation may be separated from the regulation of financial consumer protection. Competition is also a key part of consumer protection because it creates a mechanism that rewards better performers and increases the power that consumers can exert in the marketplace.
- **Governments can also subsidize access to finance and undertake other direct policies to enhance financial inclusion, but more evidence on the effectiveness of these approaches is needed.** Financial exclusion is often a result of high debt levels, especially in rural economies. Debt restructuring may be preferable to unconditional debt relief to minimize the incentives for moral hazard and restore financial inclusion.

CHAPTER FOUR

FINANCIAL INCLUSION IN INDIA

India is a nation of 1.2 billion people, spread across 29 states and seven union territories. There are around 6, 00,000 villages and 640 districts in our country. Forty per cent of the households in India have bank accounts, but only 38 per cent of the 87,051 branches of scheduled commercial banks are in rural areas. A vast majority of our population, especially in rural areas, is excluded from the easy access to finance. Efforts have been made to provide financial services, especially credit facilities, to the rural population since the 18th century. Taccavi loans were provided to the poor farmers in order to buy seeds and agricultural implements. The institutionalization of systems for financial inclusion in India began with the establishment of credit cooperatives following the enactment of the Cooperative Credit Societies Act in 1904. After Independence, these efforts were intensified, following the recommendations of the All India Rural Credit Survey Committee of 1954. The expansion of the traditional commercial banks to rural areas commenced with the nationalization of the Imperial Bank of India and its conversion to the State Bank of India in 1955. The nationalization of 14 major commercial banks in 1969 and another six commercial banks in 1980, along with the introduction of the Lead Bank Scheme in 1970, were steps that facilitated rapid expansion of the banking system into 'hitherto unbanked areas.' Regional rural banks (RRBs) were established under the RRBs Act, 1976, to overcome the difficulties faced by commercial banks, like cultural barriers in dealing with rural people and the high costs involved in the setting up of rural branches. In Bangladesh, Micro Finance Institutions (MFIs), particular "Grameen Bank" is playing a very important role to enhance the financial inclusion. RRBs were envisaged as hybrid banks, incorporating the technical competence and professionalism of the commercial banking system with the local field-level knowledge and low-cost structure of the cooperative banking system. The issues of outreach and credit were fundamental and integral to the concept of RRBs. The creation of the National Bank for Agriculture and Rural Development (NABARD) in 1982 was specifically intended to extend credit and financial services to farmers and the rural population. The cooperatives, which had made sufficient in Poverty and exclusion, continue to dominate socio-economic and political discourse in India as they have done over the last six decades in the post-independence period. Poverty reduction has been an important goal of development policy since the inception of planning in India. Various anti-poverty, employment generation and basic services programmes have been in operation for decades in India. The ongoing reforms attach great importance to removal of poverty and to addressing the wide variations across states. Though the Indian economy recorded impressive growth rates until recently, its impact has sadly not fully percolated to the lowest deciles. Despite being one of the ten fastest growing economies of the world, India is still home to one-third of the world's poor.

The Reserve Bank of India setup a commission (Khan Commission) in 2004 to look into Financial Inclusion and the recommendations of the commission were incorporated into the Mid-term review of the policy (2005-06). In the report RBI exhorted the banks with a view of achieving greater Financial Inclusion to make available a basic "no-frills" banking account. In India, Financial Inclusion first featured in 2005, when it was introduced, that, too, from a pilot project in UT of Pondicherry, by Dr. K. C. Chakraborthy, the chairman of Indian Bank. Mangalam Village became the first village in India where all households were provided banking facilities. Financial inclusion gained prime importance since 2005 when Rangarajan Committee was set up to review the banking practices hindering inclusive growth. India recognized the need for inclusive growth at the onset of independence. Unfortunately, in spite of having a far-fetched vision and well intended policies, she is still struggling to achieve its goal of financial inclusion.

The appointment of the Committee on Banking Sector Reforms (R Narasimhan) in 1998, the Committee on Financial Inclusion (C. Rangarajan) in 2007, and the agriculture debt waiver and debt relief scheme introduced by the Government of India in 2008 have further pushed the cause of financial inclusion.

The appointment of the Committee in developing economies like India, the banks, as mobilizer of savings and allocators of credit for production and investment, have a very critical role. As a financial intermediary, the banks contribute to the economic growth of the country by identifying the entrepreneurs with the best chances of successfully initiating new commercial activities and allocating credit to them. At a minimum, all retail commercial banks also provide remittance facilities and other payment related products. Thus, inherently, the banking sector possesses a tremendous potential to act as an agent of change and ensure redistribution of wealth in the society.

However, it is disheartening to note that the number of people with access to the products and services offered by the banking system continues to be very limited even years after introduction of inclusive banking initiatives in the country through measures such as the cooperative movement, nationalization of banks, creation of regional rural banks, etc. As Nobel Laureate Prof. Amartya Sen has also noted, "the thrust of developmental policy in India has undergone a paradigm shift from an exclusive focus on efficiency to one on equity; from the rate and pattern of growth, and on inequalities, distribution of income and wealth to the extent to which people are deprived of the requirements for leading a fulfilling life and suffer „capability deprivation". Over the past five years, Reserve Bank of India, as also other policy makers have resolutely pursued the agenda of financial inclusion and achieved discernible progress in improving access to financial services for the masses. The importance of financial inclusion has been emphatically underlined in the wake of the financial crisis. The crisis has had a significant negative impact on lives of individuals globally. Millions of people have lost their livelihoods, their homes and savings. One of the prominent reasons for the crisis was that the financial system was focused on furthering its own interests and lost its linkage to the real sector and with the society at large. The crisis also resulted in a realization that free market forces do not always result in greater efficiency in the financial system, particularly while protecting the interests of the vulnerable sections of society. This is due to the information asymmetry working against these sections, thereby placing them at a severe disadvantage. In wake of the crisis, therefore, Financial Inclusion has emerged as a policy imperative for inclusive growth in several countries across the globe. However, though much lip service has been paid to Financial Inclusion, the actual progress has remained far from satisfactory. It is regrettable that the entire debate surrounding financial inclusion has generated significant heat and sound, but little light.

The average population per branch office decreased from 64,000 to 18,000 as on June 2009. However, there are certain under-banked states such as Bihar, Orissa, Rajasthan, Uttar Pradesh, Chhattisgarh, Jharkhand and West Bengal where the branches are unevenly spread. The extent of financial exclusion is 75 per cent or more in the North Eastern states of Meghalaya, Arunachal Pradesh, Mizoram, Manipur and Assam.

The bank nationalization phase in India marked a paradigm shift in Indian banking, as it was intended to shift the focus from class banking to mass banking. Branches of commercial banks and RRBs have increased from 8321 in 1969 to 100,277 as on December 31, 2012. However, the progress is far from satisfactory as evidenced by the World Bank Findex Survey (2012). According to the survey findings, only 35% of Indian adults had access to a formal bank account and 8% borrowed formally in the last 12 months. Only 2% of adults used an account to receive money from a family member living in another area and 4% used an account to receive payment from the Government. The miniscule numbers suggest a crying need for a further push to the financial inclusion agenda to ensure that the people at the bottom of the pyramid join the formal financial system, reap benefits and improve their financial well-being.

There are 67 RRBs in India with a total network of 16,000 branches as on January 2013. The introduction of a universal and targeted public distribution system (PDS), the provision for employment in rural areas through the National Rural Employment Guarantee Scheme (NREGS), the implementation of the project to bring the population under a unique identification number (AADHAR) and the Direct Benefit Transfer (DBT) scheme in 2013 are the most recent measures by the government to realize inclusive growth targets.

Global Experience in Promoting Financial Inclusion

Nowadays, enhancement of financial inclusion is the main objective of every country's financial policy. The United Kingdom was one of the first countries to realise the importance of financial inclusion and has established a Financial Inclusion Fund to promote the same and assigned responsibility to banks and credit unions in removing financial exclusion. In United States of America, the "Community Reinvestment Act-(1977)" has been enacted to contribute to financial inclusion and it prohibits discrimination by banks against families with low and moderate incomes. During 2003, legislation entitled "Access to Basic Banking Services Regulations" was introduced in Canada to ensure that all Canadians could obtain personal bank accounts without difficulty. In South Africa, "MZANSI" a low cost national bank account was launched in October 2004 extending banking services to low income segments and especially to that segment for which the banking services were elusive till recently. Chaia et al. (2010) using cross-country data from previous research studies estimate the size of the world's adult population that doesn't use formal (and semi-formal) financial services. They find that over half of the world's population (2.5 billion adults) do not use formal financial services for either saving or borrowing purposes and that nearly 90 percent of this population lives in Asia, Africa, Latin America and the Middle East.

India's Experience in Promoting Financial Inclusion

Since independence Government had been thinking of financial inclusion but it took steps for its implementation on war footing much later. The process of financial inclusion in India can broadly be classified into three phases. During the First Phase (1960-1990), the focus was on channeling of credit to the neglected sectors of the economy. Special emphasis was also laid on weaker sections of the society. The second Phase (1990-2005) focused mainly on strengthening the financial institutions as part of financial sector reforms. During the Third Phase (2005 onwards), the financial inclusion was explicitly made as a policy objective and thrust was on providing the safe facility of savings deposits.

There are several benchmarks employed to assess the penetration of financial services in a country. For instance, the quantum of current and savings account (CASA) deposits held as a ratio to the adult population can be used to measure the reach of financial inclusion within a specific country, or to compare it to other countries.

According to the 2001 Census, India's CASA ratio to the total adult population was 59.

Even within the country there was a huge disparity among states. The ratio for Kerala was 89, while that for Bihar was 33. The northern region (Haryana, Chandigarh and Delhi) had a high coverage ratio of 84, compared to the meager coverage ratio of 21 for Nagaland and 27 for Manipur.

Historically, the Reserve Bank of India (RBI) and the Government of India have been making efforts to increase banking penetration in the country. Notwithstanding various improvements, financial inclusion found a place in the every financial policy of the RBI. The RBI has undertaken number of measures with the objective of attracting the financially excluded population into the structured financial system. In addition to these, some of the other major initiatives taken by RBI and Government are as follows: Opening of No Frills Accounts, Easier Credit facility by introducing a General Purpose Credit Card facility up to Rs.25,000, Simpler 'Know Your Customer' (KYC) procedure, Use of Information Technology, implementation of Business Correspondent (BC) Model and Project Financial Literacy, Financial Literacy and Credit Counseling programme and establishment of Financial Inclusion Fund.

Comparison of India with Other Countries

India and the UK are at the forefront of such efforts, and both have made key strides in supporting and enabling banks, post offices, insurers and credit providers to offer services to all their citizens. Both countries have established bodies specifically to tackle the issues of financial inclusion, setting ambitious targets. In the UK, the Financial Inclusion Taskforce oversees over £250 million of government spending and measures progress towards targets for delivering banking services, credit and debt advice. The Indian Committee on Financial Inclusion is headed by Sri C. Rangarajan, the Chairman of the Economic Advisory Council to the Indian Prime Minister. India's National Rural Financial Inclusion Plan aims to reach at least 50 per cent, or 56 million, of financially excluded households by 2012 through rural/semi-urban branches of commercial and regional rural banks, with full inclusion to be achieved by 2015.

Both countries have also made significant progress. In India, the number of "no-frills" accounts with low or nil minimum balances rose from around half a million accounts in March 2006 to 15 million in 2008, with smart cards accounting for two to three million of these accounts. Meanwhile, the existing branch network in India 45,000 rural and semi-urban branches has enabled public sector banks and the regional rural banks to scale up their efforts by leveraging on the existing capacity.

Both India and UK recognize that by encouraging and supporting people to manage their finances, they can reduce the impact of poverty and help families to sustain themselves, start small businesses and allow enterprise to flourish. They realize that excluding those on low incomes from financial services creates a lack of cash flow for poor families, recourse to expensive moneylenders and the inability to save for emergencies such as sickness and poor harvests, or for older age.

The UK Government and industry are already working in partnership with India to build on our shared experience of encouraging financial inclusion through making bank accounts more accessible, extending credit facilities, and supporting microfinance initiatives and self-help groups.

Many UK companies have also shown their commitment to promoting financial inclusion in India, particularly to the rural poor, by striving to extend the accessibility of financial products such as bank accounts and microfinance to all.

"UK companies are in India for the long-term," says Vicki Treadell, British Deputy High Commissioner based in Mumbai. "They see their role as playing an important part in fuelling the growth of the Indian economy not just servicing successful metropolitan companies but also reaching out to ordinary people. By following programmes of branch expansion, improving financial literacy and leveraging IT solutions to extend reach, they are demonstrating their determination to make financial services available to all."

Around the world, there is more attention than ever to the ways in which access to financial services accelerates progress toward development and the persisting needs we still face. This has spurred a first wave of high-level commitments by governments, international agencies, the private sector, and others to make the vision of financial inclusion a reality. G20 leaders recognized financial inclusion as a cross-cutting issue for development and economic system stability, and included it in work plans. In 2012, 17 countries committed to create cross-sector coordination platforms and national strategies under the G20 and the AFI Maya Declaration has gained over 30 commitments from national regulators and policy makers. Unique partnerships are forming, for example the Better than Cash Alliance brings together private sector, donors and governments to advance the use of digital channels. ASEAN leaders recognized financial inclusion as a key to inclusive and sustained growth for the region, and global standard setters have incorporated financial inclusion considerations into their guidelines for banking regulation and supervision.

The extent of financial services outreach is very low in India especially when compared with developed countries. For instance, 92-94 per cent population of the UK either has a current or savings bank account. The Reserve Bank of India (RBI) has actively sought to address this problem with a slew of measures, including a new licensing policy for banks that mandates 25 per cent of their branches must be opened in rural areas that are largely excluded from the mainstream financial economy.

Present Status of Financial Inclusion in India

In order to study the important aspects of financial inclusion it is important to know the method to measure the financial inclusion. There are many methods for measurement of financial inclusion but according to Thorat (2006) one common measure of financial inclusion is the percentage of adults with bank accounts (deposit and credit). A study by Chakrabarty (2006) showed that in India there are 17 credit accounts and 54 saving accounts per 100 persons and at the same time only 13 percent people are availing loans from the banks in the income bracket of less than Rs. 50000 per annum. Leeladhar's (2006) study revealed that one of the benchmarks employed to assess the degree of reach of financial services to the population of the country, is the quantum of deposit accounts (current and savings) held as a ratio to the adult population. In Indian context, taking into account the census of 2001, the ratio of deposit accounts to the total adult population was only 59 percent. But within the country, there is a wide variation across states. For instance, the ratio for the state of Kerala is as high as 89 percent while Bihar is marked by a low coverage of 33 percent. A study by Sharma (2007) has evolved a concept of "Index of Financial Inclusion" to make it a more comprehensive indicator of inclusion in an economy. The index is an amalgamation of three aspects of the financial inclusion; penetration of the banking system, its availability to users and its actual usage. All these aspects are measured by using data on number of bank accounts per hundred population, number of bank branches per thousand populations and the size of bank credit and deposits relative to the GDP respectively. According to this study in the group of 100 countries, India's rank was 50 while Spain's and Switzerland's ranks were first and fifth respectively. Sangwan (2008) revealed that as on 31st March 2006 in India the saving accounts per 100 adult populations were 63 and credit accounts were only 16. Conory (2008) pointed out that the exclusion of people from financial services is a general problem, to which microfinance is one of the possible solution. It is a powerful tool for achieving higher levels of financial inclusion efficiency and equity benefits in developing economies. Subbarao (2010) pointed out that efforts at financial inclusion are not new; both the government and RBI have been pursuing this goal over the last several decades through building the rural cooperative structure in the 1950s, the social contract with banks in the 1960s and the expansion of bank branch network in the 1970s and 1980s. These initiatives have paid off in terms of a network of branches across the country. Yet the extent of financial exclusion is staggering and the RBI approach to financial inclusion aims at 'connecting people' with the banking system and not just opening accounts. Lyngdoh and Pati (2010) concluded that microfinance based financial inclusion has ensured that the underprivileged and downtrodden are taken special care of. It has led to their economic empowerment and subsequently in socio-political development outcomes i.e. inclusive growth. Gokarn (2011) observed that the process of financial inclusion is going to be incomplete and inadequate if it is measured only in term of new accounts being opened and operated. Actually a huge proportion of the Indian workforce is either self-employed or in the causal labour segment which suggests the need for products that will make access to credit easier to the former, while offering opportunities for risk mitigation and consumption smoothing to the latter.

India is one country where the Financial Stability and Development Council (FSDC) has a specific mandate for financial inclusion and financial literacy. There is a separate Technical Group on Financial Inclusion and Financial Literacy under the aegis of FSDC with representation from all the financial sector regulators.

In order to spearhead efforts towards greater financial inclusion, RBI has constituted a Financial Inclusion Advisory Committee (FIAC) under the Chairmanship of a Deputy Governor from RBI. The FIAC has few Directors from the Central Board of RBI and experts drawn from NGO sector/other civil society representatives, etc. as members. The collective expertise and experience of the members is expected to be leveraged to explore issues such as developing viable and sustainable banking services delivery models focusing on accessible and affordable financial services, developing products and processes for rural as well as urban unbanked consumers.

At the state level, we have State Level Bankers Committees (SLBC) in all the states. Going further down, we have Lead District Managers in all the 659 districts, with recent inclusion of the metropolitan areas into the Lead Banks Scheme.

About 700 financial literacy centres have been set up by banks. There are Rural Self-Employment Training Institutes (R-SETI), working towards capacity building for taking up self employment ventures.

In India RBI have encouraged banks to adopt a structured and planned approach to financial inclusion with commitment at the highest levels, through preparation of Board approved Financial Inclusion Plans (FIPs). The first phase of Financial Inclusion Plans was implemented over the period 2010-2013. The Reserve Bank has sought to use the Financial Inclusion Plans as the basis for Financial Inclusion initiatives at the bank level. Reserve Bank has put in place a structured, comprehensive monitoring mechanism for evaluating banks" performance against their Financial Inclusion Plans. Annual review meetings are being held with CMDs of banks to ensure top management support and commitment to the Financial Inclusion process.

Self Help Groups (SHGs) are playing a very important role in the process of financial inclusion. A most notable milestone in the Self Help Groups movement was when NABARD launched the pilot phase of the SHG Bank Linkage programme in February 1992. The Self Help Groups movement in India has enabled social and economic inclusion of people. The Self Help Groups Bank Linkage movement, where SHGs are linked to banks in a gradual way-initially through savings and later through loan products, has been able to ensure financial inclusion to a certain extent. The Self Help Groups have become the common vehicle of development process covering all development programmes. The number of Self Help Groups banks linked in India increased from 255 in 1992-93 to 1609586 in 2008-09. In the same way loan disbursed to these Self Help Groups increased from Rs.0.29 crore in 1992-93 to Rs. 12253.51 crore in 2008-09. Thus, from 1992-93 to 2008-09 the number of SHGs have increased by 6312 times and the bank's loan disbursement to 42253.48 times. During 2008-09, the commercial banks had lead in disbursement of loan to Self Help Groups with 62.4 percent share followed by RRBs with 25.2 percent and co-operative banks with a share of 12.4 per cent. During the same year commercial banks disbursed Rs. 8060.53 crore (65.8 percent) to 1004587 SHGs, RRBs Rs. 3193.49 crore (26.1 percent) to 405569 SHGs and co-operative banks Rs. 999.49 crore (8.2 percent) to 199430 SHGs.

Progress made by Banks under the Financial Inclusion Plans (April 2010 – March 2013)

A snapshot of the progress made by banks under the Financial Inclusion Plans (April 2010 – March 2013) for key parameters, during the three year period is as under:

- Nearly 2, 68, 000 banking outlets have been set up in villages as on March 13 as against 67,694 banking outlets in villages in March 2010
- About 7400 rural branches opened during this period
- Nearly 109 million Basic Savings Bank Deposit Accounts (BSBDAs) have been added, taking the total no. of BSBDAs to 182 million. Share of ICT based accounts have increased substantially – Percentage of ICT accounts to total BSBDAs has increased from 25percent in March 10 to 45percent in March 13
- With the addition of nearly 9.48 million farm sector households during this period, 33.8 million households have been provided with small entrepreneurial credit as at the end of March 2013
- With the addition of nearly 2.25 million non farm sector households during this period, 3.6 million households have been provided with small entrepreneurial credit as at the end of March 2013.
- About 4904 lakh transactions have been carried out in ICT based accounts through BCs during the three year period

It is important to analyze this progress against some disconcerting trends that were noticed in the run up to the structured Financial Inclusion initiatives that the banks launched since 2010 onwards. First, the number of banked centres in the country between 1991 and 2007 had actually come down (from 35236 to 34471). Second, the number of rural branches during the same period had also declined significantly (from 35206 to 30409).

Against this backdrop, the progress made during 2010-13 is certainly remarkable. In order to continue with the process of ensuring access to banking services to the excluded, banks have now been advised to draw up a fresh 3 year Financial Inclusion Plan for the period 2013-16. Banks have also been advised that the FIPs prepared by them are disaggregated and percolated down up to the branch level. The disaggregation of the plans is being done with a view to ensure involvement of bank staff across the hierarchy, in the FI efforts and also to ensure uniformity in the reporting structure under the Financial Inclusion Plan. The focus is also now more on the volume of transactions in new accounts opened as a part of the financial inclusion drive.

Major Schemes for Financial Inclusion in India

1. **National Mission on Financial Inclusion**
    - The Committee feels that the task of financial inclusion must be taken up in a mission mode as a financial inclusion plan at the national level.
    - A National Mission on Financial Inclusion (NaMFI) comprising representatives from all stakeholders may be constituted to aim at achieving universal financial inclusion within a specific time frame.

- The Mission should be responsible for suggesting the overall policy changes required for achieving the desired level of financial inclusion, and for supporting a range of stakeholders – in the domain of public, private and NGO sectors - in undertaking promotional initiatives.

1. **National Rural Financial Inclusion Plan (NRFIP)**

- A National Rural Financial Inclusion Plan (NRFIP) may be launched with a clear target to provide access to comprehensive financial services, including credit, to at least 50% of financially excluded households, say 55.77 million by 2012 through rural/semi-urban branches of Commercial Banks and Regional Rural Banks.

- The remaining households, with such shifts as may occur in the rural/urban population, have to be covered by 2015.

- Semi-urban and rural branches of commercial banks and RRBs may set for themselves a minimum target of covering 250 new cultivator and non-cultivator households per branch per annum, with an emphasis on financing marginal farmers and poor non-cultivator households.

3. **Handling Cost through Funds**

- There is a cost involved in this massive exercise of extending financial services to hitherto excluded segments of population. Such costs may come down over a period of time with the resultant business expansion.

- However, in the initial stages some funding support is required for promotional and developmental initiatives that will lead to better credit absorption capacity among the poor and vulnerable sections and for application of technology for facilitating the mandated levels of inclusion.

- The Committee has, therefore, proposed the constitution of two funds with NABARD – the Financial Inclusion Promotion & Development Fund and the Financial Inclusion Technology Fund with an initial corpus of Rs. 500 crore each to be contributed in equal proportion by GoI/RBI/NABARD. This recommendation has already been accepted by the Government of India.

4. **Business Correspondent Model**

- The Rangarajan Committee recommended that extending outreach on a scale envisaged under NRFIP would be possible only by leveraging technology to open up channels beyond branch network.

- Adoption of appropriate technology would enable the branches to go where the customer is present instead of the other way round. This, however, is in addition to extending traditional mode of banking by targeted branch expansion in identified districts.

- The Business Facilitator/Business Correspondent (BF/BC) models riding on appropriate technology can deliver this outreach and should form the core of the strategy for extending financial inclusion.

- The Committee has made some recommendations for relaxation of norms for expanding the coverage of BF/BC. Ultimately, banks should Endeavour to have a BC touch point in each of the 6, 00,000 villages in the country.

5. **Procedural Simplification**

- Procedural Changes like simplifying mortgage requirements, exemption from Stamp Duty for loans to small and marginal farmers and providing agricultural / business development services in the farm and non-farm sectors respectively will help in extending financial inclusion.

6. **New Role of Regional Rural Banks (RRBs)**

   - Regional Rural Banks, post -merger, represent a powerful instrument for financial inclusion. Their outreach vis-à-vis other scheduled commercial banks particularly in regions and across population groups facing the brunt of financial exclusion is impressive.

   - RRBs account for 37 per cent of total rural offices of all scheduled commercial banks and 91 per cent of their workforce is posted in rural and semi-urban areas.

   - They account for 31 per cent of deposit accounts and 37 per cent of loan accounts in rural areas.

   - Regional Rural Banks have a large presence in regions marked by financial exclusion of a high order.

- They account for 34 per cent of all branches in North-Eastern, 30 per cent in Eastern and 32 per cent in Central regions.

- Out of the total 22.38 lakh Self Help Group Bank Linkage Scheme credit linked by the banking industry as on 31st March 2006, 33 per cent of the linkages were by RRBs which is quite impressive to say the least.

- Significantly the more backward the region the greater is the share of Regional Rural Banks which is amply demonstrated by their 56 per cent share in the North-Eastern, 48 per cent in Central and 40 per cent in Eastern region.

- RRBs are, thus, the best suited vehicles to widen and deepen the process of financial inclusion. However, there has to be a firm reinforcement of the rural orientation of these institutions with a specific mandate on financial inclusion.

- The Committee recommended that the process of merger of RRBs should not proceed beyond the level of sponsor bank in each State. The Committee has also recommended the recapitalization of RRBs with negative Net Worth and widening of their network to cover all unbanked villages in the districts where they are operating, either by opening a branch or through the BF/BC model in a time bound manner. Their area of operation may also be extended to cover the 87 districts, presently not covered by them.

Self Help Group Bank Linkage Scheme

There are a large number of SHGs in the country which are well established in their savings and credit operations. The members of such groups want to expand and diversify their activities with a view to attain economies of scale. Many of the groups are organizing themselves into federations and other higher level structures. To achieve this effectively, resource centres can play a vital role. Federations of Self Help Group at village and taluk levels have certain advantages. Federations, if they emerge voluntarily from amongst SHGs, can be encouraged. However, the Committee felt that they cannot be entrusted with the financial intermediation function.

- The Committee has recommended amendment to NABARD Act to enable it to provide micro finance services to the urban poor.

Joint Liability Groups

- Self Help Group Bank bank linkage has emerged as an effective credit delivery channel to the poor clients. However, there are segments within the poor such as share croppers/oral lessees/tenant farmers, whose loan requirements are much larger but who have no collaterals to fit into the traditional financing approaches of the banking system.

- To service such clients, Joint Liability Groups (JLGs), an upgradation of Self Help Group Bank model, could be an effective way. NABARD had piloted a project for formation and linking of JLGs during 2004-05 in 8 States of the country through 13 RRBs.

Based on the encouraging response from the project, a scheme for financing JLGs of tenant farmers and oral lessees has also been evolved. The Committee has recommended that adoption of the Joint Liability Groups concept could be another effective method for purveying credit to mid-segment clients such as small farmers, marginal farmers, tenant farmers, etc. and thereby reduce their dependence on informal sources of credit.

Micro Finance Institutions - Non Banking Finance Companies

- The committee recommended a greater legitimacy, accountability and transparency for Micro Finance Institutions which only enable MFIs to source adequate debt and equity funds, but also eventually enable them to take and use savings as a low cost source for on-lending.

- The committee also recommended that there was a need to recognize a separate category of Micro finance – Non Banking Finance Companies (MF–NBFCs), without any relaxation on start-up capital and subject to the regulatory prescriptions applicable for Non Banking Finance Companies. Such Micro Finance Institutions could provide thrift, credit, micro-insurance, remittances and other financial services up to a specified amount to the poor in rural, semi-urban and urban areas.

- Such Micro finance – Non Banking Finance Companies may also be recognized as Business Correspondents of banks for providing only savings and remittance services and also act as micro insurance agents.

Cooperative System

In terms of number of agricultural credit accounts, the Short Term Cooperative Credit System (STCCS) has 50% more accounts than the commercial banks and RRBs put together.

- On an average, there is one Primary Agricultural Societies for every 6 villages; these societies have a total membership of more than 120 million rural people making it one of the largest rural financial systems in the world.

- However, the health of a very large proportion of these rural credit cooperatives has deteriorated significantly.

For this segment, the Rangarajan Committee reiterated the need to implement the recommendation of the Vaidyanathan Committee Report, which had suggested an implementable Action Plan with substantial financial assistance.

Concluding Remarks

On the basis of above discussion it may be concluded that despite significant growth of financial sector in India a vast segment of population especially low income groups or underprivileged section of society have not been covered under financial inclusion. Availability of banking services to the entire population without any discrimination is the prime objective of financial inclusion. In India there are many reasons for financial exclusion and it may bring many negative effects on individual as well as on the society. The main reason for low financial inclusion are lack of adequate supportive infrastructure, absence of appropriate technology, financial illiteracy, lack of suitable financial products and its inflexibility. The Reserve Bank of India and Government of India has been making many efforts to increase financial inclusion. The emergence of Self Help Group as financial intermediaries in recent year has raised hopes that excluded people and rural India could be effectively financial linked. The Self Help Group Bank Linkage Programme is playing a very important role in the process of financial inclusion in India. Keeping in view the role of financial inclusion in the process of inclusive growth, its effective expansion is a must. When people become aware of the proper use and benefits of the financial services they start getting themselves associated with the development schemes run by the government and others. This has a positive impact on the process of inclusive growth. Financial inclusion is a necessary condition for inclusive growth and in order to achieve it, we should remove or reduce all regional imbalance of financial infrastructure. Financial inclusion should be used as a tool for inclusive growth and Banks, and Micro Finance Institutions, and Non Government Organisations can play a simultaneous major role to achieve it. Banks should redesign their business strategies to incorporate specific plans to promote financial inclusion of low income group treating it both as a business opportunity and as a corporate social responsibility. Banks should also ensure wide publicity about their financial products and policies to enhance financial literacy.

CHAPTER FIVE

DIMENSION OF FINANCIAL INCLUSION IN INDIA

Indian economy has changed a lot over the past 60 years. Over the next 40 years the changes could be dramatic. Using the latest demographic projection and a model of capital accumulation and productivity growth, we map out GDP growth in the Indian economy until 2050. The result shows that if things go right, the Indian economy could become an important source of growth to the world economy. Our projections are optimistic, in the sense that they assume reasonably successful development Any kind of long term projection is subject to a great deal of uncertainty, and we need to be mindful that India's growth transition is unlikely to be smooth or devoid of shocks.

Households in developing countries such as India require finance for a variety of reasons, consumption, and meeting lump-sum expenses like a marriage or illness and most importantly for income-generating activities. Since credit is essential for meeting critical needs, an access to credit is crucial for maintaining and improving social and economic condition of households. Therefore, adequate credit at reasonable cost is important for socio-economic development. So, a well settled and even distributed banking sector is the first need for the purpose of financial inclusion as only formal agencies of credit are able to fulfill both condition i.e., to meet the need of demand of credit for households at an adequate level and at low cost. Many studies argue that 'access to safe, easy and affordable credit and other financial services by the poor and vulnerable groups, disadvantaged areas and lagging sectors are recognized as a pre-condition for accelerating growth and reducing income disparities and poverty'.

According to United Nation 'Access to a well-functioning financial system, by creating equal opportunities, enables economically and socially excluded people to integrate better into the economy and actively contribute to development and protect themselves against economic shocks'. Despite the broad international consensus regarding the importance of access to finance as a crucial poverty alleviation tool, it is estimated that globally over two billion people are currently excluded from access to financial services (United Nations, 2006a). In most developing countries, a large segment of society, particularly low-income people, has very little access to financial services, both formal and semi-formal. As a consequence, many of them have to necessarily depend either on their own or informal sources of finance and generally at an unreasonably high cost. The situation is worse in most least developed countries (LDCs), where more than 90 per cent of the population is excluded from access to the formal financial system (United Nations, 2006a).

On the basis of the given review of literature, the researcher identified four parameters to analyze impact of Financial Inclusions, namely; Bank Branches, Credit Account, Savings Account, and Credit-Deposit Ratio.

Through this chapter researcher discusses the relationship between financial inclusion and development with the help of index of financial inclusion and the chapter also explores the factors associated with financial inclusion with the help of Regression Analysis. For this purpose, 15 Indian States were selected out of 28 states, and 6 Union Territories.

The index of financial inclusion was developed by Sarma in 2008. According to this index, financial inclusion is a measure of inclusiveness of the financial sector of a country. It is constructed as a multidimensional index that captures information on various aspects of financial inclusion such as banking penetration, availability of banking services and usage of the banking system. The IFI incorporates information on these dimensions in one single number lying between 0 and 1, where 0 denotes complete financial exclusion and 1 indicates complete financial inclusion in an economy.

For Thorat (2006) one common measure of financial inclusion is the percentage of adults with bank accounts (deposit and credit). A study by Chakrabarty (2006) showed that in India there are 17 credit accounts and 54 saving accounts per 100 persons and at the same time only 13 percent people are availing loans from the banks in the income bracket of less than Rs. 50000 per annum. Leeladhar's (2006) study revealed that one of the benchmarks employed to assess the degree of reach of financial services to the population of the country, is the quantum of deposit accounts (current and savings) held as a ratio to the adult population. In Indian context, taking into account the census of 2001, the ratio of deposit accounts to the total adult population was only 59 percent. But within the country, there is a wide variation across states. For instance, the ratio for the state of Kerala is as high 89 percent while Bihar is marked by a low coverage of 33 percent. A study by Sharma (2007) has evolved a concept of "Index of Financial Inclusion" to make it a more comprehensive indicator of inclusion in an economy. The index is an amalgamation of three aspects of the financial inclusion; penetration of the banking system, its availability to users and its actual usage. All these aspects are measured by using data on number of bank accounts per hundred population, number of bank branches per thousand populations and the size of bank credit and deposits relative to the GDP respectively. According to this study in the group of 100 countries, India's rank was 50 while Spain's and Switzerland's ranks were first and fifth respectively.

Sangwan (2008) revealed that as on 31st March 2006 in India the saving accounts per 100 adult populations were 63 and credit accounts were only 16. Conory (2008) pointed out that the exclusion of people from financial services is a general problem, to which microfinance is one of the possible solution. It is a powerful tool for achieving higher levels of financial inclusion efficiency and equity benefits in developing economies. Subbarao (2010) pointed out that efforts at financial inclusion are not new; both the government and RBI have been pursuing this goal over the last several decades through building the rural cooperative structure in the 1950s, the social contract with banks in the 1960s and the expansion of bank branch network in the 1970s and 1980s. These initiatives have paid off in terms of a network of branches across the country. Yet the extent of financial exclusion is staggering and the RBI approach to financial inclusion aims at 'connecting people' with the banking system and not just opening accounts.

Lyngdoh and Pati (2010) concluded that microfinance based financial inclusion has ensured that the underprivileged and downtrodden are taken special care of. It has led to their economic empowerment and subsequently in socio-political development outcomes i.e. inclusive growth. Gokarn (2011) observed that the process of financial inclusion is going to be incomplete and inadequate if it is measured only in term of new accounts being opened and operated. Actually a huge proportion of the Indian workforce is either self-employed or in the casual labour segment which suggests the need for products that will make access to credit easier to the former, while offering opportunities for risk mitigation and consumption smoothing to the latter.

Dimension of Index of Financial Inclusion

1. **Accessibility**: Accessibility has been measured by the penetration of the bankingsystem given by the number of bank A/C, per 1,000 populations.
2. **Availability**: Availability has been measured by the number of bank branches andnumber of ATMs per 1, 00,000 people.
3. **Uses:** The volumes of credit plus deposit are related to the GDP.

A dimension index for each of these dimensions has been first computed by the following formula

dij= Aij-mi/Mi-mi..(1)

Where:

Aij = Actual value of dimension i and state j, mi = minimum value of dimension i and state j, Mi = maximum value of dimension i and j state.

After calculating and compilation of the above three dimension i.e., penetration, availability and usage, we can represent a state ij by a point (pij, aij, uij) in the three dimensional Cartesian space, such that 0 ≤ pij, aij, uij ≤1, where pij, aij and uij denote the each dimension indexes for each state ij computed using formula (1).

After calculate the individual dimensions value of each state, we have applied 2nd equation/ formula. The 2nd formula is given below:

IFI = $\sqrt{}$ (1-pi) + (1-a1) + (1-ui)/3........................ (2)

The IFI for the state ij is measured by the normalized inverse Euclidean distance of the point (pij, aij, uij) from the ideal point (1). The normalization is done in order to make the value lie between 0 and 1 and the inverse distance is considered so that higher value of the IFI corresponds to higher financial inclusion.

Categorize among of Results on the base of IFI

On the basis of IFI value, all considered states have been categorized into three categories i.e.,

- $0.5 < IFI \leq 1$ – high financial inclusion
- $0.3 \leq IFI < 0.5$ – medium financial inclusion
- $0 \leq IFI < 0.3$ – low financial inclusion

Multiple Regression Equation Model

Multiple regressions represent a logical extension of more than two variables regression analysis. Instead, more than one independent and one dependent variable is used to estimate the values of a dependent variables. The multiple regression equation describes the averages relationship among more than two variables and this relationship is used to predict or control the dependent variables. The formula for calculating multiple regressions is as follow:

The general form of the regression equation is:

$Y = a_0 + a_1X_1 + a_2X_2 + \ldots a_nX_n + \varepsilon$ .... (3)

Where X_1, X_2 etc are regressed variables, a_1, a_2 and so on are the parameters to be estimated from the data and ε is the error term following classical OLS assumptions i.e., The deviations ε is assumed to be independent and normally distributed with mean 0 and standard deviation (σ).

In the regression equations, the dependent variable is a logit transformation of the index of financial inclusion described earlier. Unlike the IFI which lies between 0 and 1, the transformed variable lies between $-\infty$ and ∞. This allows us to carry out the classical OLS regression. The transformed variable is a monotonically increasing function of IFI, and hence it preserves the same ordering as IFI. The transformed variable is a logit function of the original variable IFI, as defined below.

Y = IFI (IFI/1- IFI)... (4)

In research, we have framed four regression equations i.e., the first regression measure the degree of relation between development and financial inclusion, second equation measures the degree of relation between economic development and financial inclusion, third describes the relation between economic development indicator and financial inclusion and the last highlights the relation between socio economic development and financial inclusion.

Constraints And Further Area Of Research

In financial inclusion, there are a few potentially interesting areas for future research –viz., (a) the most appropriate delivery model (which banks are still trying to figure out) for different geographical regions given their unique characteristics, (b) The unbanked segments-be it in rural, urban or metropolitan areas are largely served by the un-organized sector even today. Research into the products, practices and procedures of this unorganized sectors an absolute imperative, to identify and understand the same which the bottom of the pyramid populace finds so convenient and comfortable to deal with. This could throw up valuable leads for the organized sector–banks and financial institutions to follow (c) Further, in order to measure the intensity of money lenders especially in rural areas, research agencies should, inter alia, conduct a census of money lenders in rural India.

For implementing full financial inclusion we can opt for "Innovative Financial Inclusion"

Innovative financial inclusion means improving access to financial services for poor people through the safe and sound spread of new approaches. The following principles aim to help create an enabling policy and regulatory environment for innovative financial inclusion. The enabling environment will critically determine the speed at which the financial services access gap will close for the more than two billion people currently excluded. These principles for innovative financial inclusion derive from the experiences and lessons learned from policymakers throughout the world, especially leaders from developing countries.

- **Leadership**: Cultivate a broad-based government commitment to financial inclusion to help alleviate poverty.
- **Diversity**: Implement policy approaches that promote competition and provide market-based incentives for delivery of sustainable financial access and usage of a broad range of affordable services (savings, credit, payments and transfers, insurance) as well as a diversity of service providers.
- **Innovation**: Promote technological and institutional innovation as a means to expand financial system access and usage, including by addressing infrastructure weaknesses.
- **Protection**: Encourage a comprehensive approach to consumer protection that recognizes the roles of government, providers and consumers.
- **Empowerment**: Develop financial literacy and financial capability.
- **Cooperation**: Create an institutional environment with clear lines of accountability and coordination within government; and also encourage partnerships and direct consultation across government, business and other stakeholders.
- **Knowledge**: Utilize improved data to make evidence based policy, measure progress, and consider an incremental "test and learn" approach acceptable to both regulator and service provider.
- **Proportionality**: Build a policy and regulatory framework that is proportionate with the risks and benefits involved in such innovative products and services and is based on an understanding of the gaps and barriers in existing regulation.
- **Framework**: Consider the following in the regulatory framework, reflecting international standards, national circumstances and support for a competitive landscape: an appropriate, flexible, risk-based Anti-Money Laundering and Combating the Financing of Terrorism (AML/CFT) regime; conditions for the use of agents as a customer interface; a clear regulatory regime for electronically stored value; and market-base.

Printed by Libri Plureos GmbH in Hamburg,
Germany